Re Ignite The Fire

Re Ignite The Fire

Dr. Eric Evenhuis

Reignite the Fire

Printed in the United States of America
ISBN 978-1-967279-51-7 (hc)
ISBN 978-1-967279-49-4 (sc)
ISBN 978-1-967279-50-0 (e)

08.21.2025

This book is printed on acid-free paper.

Blue Ink Media Solutions
1111B S Governors Ave
STE 7582 Dover,
DE 19904

www.blueinkmediasolutions.com

Contents

Introduction

People are interesting! I believe that most people think about sex more often than what you might think. Sexuality is a universal phenomenon. When I told friends recently that "I'm writing my third book", their usual response is, "What's it about?" When I tell them that the title of my book is 'Reigniting the Fire', they always respond with a seductive and sly smile, their eyes get big, and their eyebrows raise, for you must know that they are thinking that this is a book about sex. When I tell them that this is a book about marital reconciliation, they become even more intrigued.

Well, the truth of the matter, is that sex in marriage is a very real part of the book. If you're the impatient type, my last chapter is indeed about sex in the final process of marital reconciliation. You may want to jump to the last chapter and read that first, but then you would miss the fun of the process of how you get to the last chapter. The last chapter deals with renewed harmony, unity, love and intimacy in marriage.

I don't believe that I need to inform anyone that the state of marriage is in serious trouble. The divorce rate in the United States is about 50 out of 100 marriages lost to divorce. In California, the rate is worse, as 2 out of every 3 marriages end in divorce. Now here's the kicker: how many of those who are still married are truly happy and functioning? I know that there are many people who are staying together in a very troubled, unhappy and sexless marriage.

I am a Pastor, (Chaplain), Marriage and Family Counselor, and all around 'good guy'. For the most part, I really like my work. I am a married man. I have been married to a most wonderful and beautiful woman for 56 years now! Her name is Nancy. We have a true love story. I am a father of two girls, and I also have seven grandchildren; and they are all amazing as well. (You can read more about my story in my previous book, "Little Ricky's Circle of Trust").

But now it's time for you to hear my confession: I don't like Marriage Counseling. It's very hard work and it often gives me a headache. Nonetheless, I am skilled at my trade and I know that I have helped to save many couples who hired me to be their counselor. I believe the reason I am effective as a Marriage Counselor is because I know and understand the road map towards reconciliation. The road map that guides me is none other than the Word of God.

The good news of the gospels is a story of God's reconciliation for His People. Did you know that God divorced His people, His wife? But God never gave up. God restored and reconciled His people to Himself, as his beautiful Bride, the Church. You would also know the agent for this reconciliation was none other than the kindest man who ever lived, Jesus, the Christ. And therefore, it was Jesus who restored and reconciled you to perfect love, perfect peace, perfect unity and pelfect intimacy now and forever more. With God there are no irreconcilable differences. I really like that idea. So now, having read my introduction, let's get on with 'Reigniting the Fire! I hope you will enjoy my book.

-Dr. Eric Evenhuis

CHAPTER I

INTRODUCTION

Theme of the book

Reconciliation in marriage is the theme of this book In the field of marriage counseling, vast amounts of time and effort have already been invested in discovering proper methods in marital reconciliation. The Family Service Association of America (FSAA) has recently printed How to Stay Married, written by Lobsenz and Blackburn (1968). This book is the result of information gained by caseworkers in FSAA agencies. authors write,

> In their book, the In 1968 alone, more than 335 agencies, in the U.S. and Canada, and their three thousand social-work counselors, served more than two million men, women, and children in over four hundred thousand families [p. 12].

Countless other agencies, churches, and professional marriage counselors have all added their time and talents to the process of healing broken and estranged relations between husbands and wives. The very fact that many efforts have been invested in reconciling marriages does, in one respect, provide an indication that marriage as an institution is deteriorating in today's society. In an attempt to gain a perspective for the breakdown of marriages, this study provides a few facts taken from the book Becoming Partners by Rogers (1972). He writes,

> In California in 1970 there were 173,000 marriages and approximately 114,000 "dissolutions of marriage." In other words, for every 100 couples who married there were 66 who were permanently parting. This is admittedly a distorted picture because a new law became effective in 1970 permitting couples to "dissolve" their marriages without trying to blame the "guilty party" simply on

the basis of agreement... So let us look at 1969. In that year for every 100 couples marrying, 49 were getting divorced... In L.A. County in 1969 divorces equaled 61 of the number of marriages. In 1970, under the law, the number of dissolutions of marriage in the county was 74 of the number of marriages. Three couples were getting their marriages dissolved while four couples were getting married! And in 1971, in L.A. County there were 61,560 marriage licenses issued and 48,221 suits filed for dissolution of marriage, 79 of that number that were marrying. Thus in 1971, for every 5 couples intending to marry, four were intending to dissolve their marriages [pp. 9-10]!

These statistics represent an alarming state of affairs in regard to marriage. In a recent best seller, Open Marriage, the O'Neills (1972) summarize society's attitude toward marriage:

The shortcomings of marriage are now being spelled out by an ever-growing legion of the divorced, the unhappily married, and the young people who, in the somber light of their elders' bitter experiences, have become wary about making any commitment to such a disaster themselves [p. 15].

In spite of these discouraging statistics and attitudes, there are those who believe that marriage is and can be an enriching life. Such concern for the broken marital relation indicates the positive value placed on marriage as it relates to the personal growth of each partner. Lobsenz and Blackburn (1968) write,

Family Service Association of America. is committed to the belief that the family has never been more important than it is today and that marriage and family life provide crucial and otherwise unobtainable psychological supports and emotional satisfactions [p. 12).

More important than the human concern for marriage is God's concern for marriage as revealed in His Word. God initiated marriage when He created the woman to be Adam's partner. "God said, 'It is not good that the man should be alone, I will make him a helper fit for him' [Genesis 2:18]."1 In addition to this, Jesus revealed the will of God for marriages when He said nothing can break what God has united. Jesus said,

> But from the beginning of creation, "God made them male and female." "For this reason a man shall leave his father and mother and be joined to his wife, and the two shall become one." So they are no longer two but one. What therefore God-has joined together, let not man put asunder [Mark 10:6-9]."

[1] The Revised Standard Version of the Bible is used whenever Scripture is quoted in this study. In various instances, Scripture depicts marriage as representing the relationship between God and His chosen people in the Old Testament and between Christ and His church in the New Testament. The fact that Scripture uses marriage as an analogy of a divine relation implies the value which God places on marriage.

In view of all the concern and the positive regard God places on marriage, the clear fact remains that there are marriages in need of reconciliation. When a man and a woman marry, they often find that they are confronted with problems, disillusionments, and, at times, alienation. If alienation does come, then there are certain processes of reconciliation through which a husband and wife need to move. Such processes of reconciliation as this study proposes to examine are based upon an investigation of the Scriptures. (Integrity Therapy has been used as a model in this study.) Scripture is not intended to be a marriage handbook nor does this study consider it as such. The Scriptures do, however, provide guidelines for married couples~particularly in the matter of reconciliation. In its broadest sense, Scripture is God's reconciling message for man in Jesus Christ. One method which Scripture uses to depict its reconciling nature is through the analogy of an alienated wife (Israel) who becomes reconciled once again to her faithful husband (God) through Jesus Christ.

Definition of Reconciliation

The word reconciliation in itself implies that some form of alienation exists with a relationship, whether between God and man, or husband and wife. In defining this term, Taylor (1951) writes,

> Reconciliation is the word used in the New Testament to describe the changed relations between God and man which are the results of the death and resurrection of Jesus Christ. Reconciliation has the significance of a new stage in personal relationships in which previous hostility of mind or estrangement has been put away in some decisive act [p. 185].

The message of reconciliation is depicted in various ways throughout Scripture. However, the concern of this study is concentrated on reconciliation as it is expressed in the marital analogy. This marital analogy is of special interest because it not only illustrates God's reconciling love to man, but it provides guidelines for marital reconciliation as well.

Uses of Analogy to Marital Therapy

In his book Kerygma and Counseling, Oden (1966) raises the question whether analogy can be applied to therapy. He has observed that, for the most part, the theological use of analogy has moved in the wrong directions; i.e., defining the divine relationship from inferences of the human situation. He writes,

> If one begins with the secular process, untheologically understood, and only then moves from there to its implications for Christian doctrines of sin, grace, etc., one has already made crucial theological decisions [p. 124].

Oden (1966) concludes that such attempts have been useful indeed as a tool for theological reflection and study. However, for those in the area of practical theology, i.e., application of theology to therapeutic usage, such studies are still forthcoming. Oden carefully lays the groundwork for such an attempt and concludes that such a task is possible. He writes,

> Without totally denying the validity of all these efforts, we intend to show that the analogy can and must be read the other way, deriving psycho-therapeutic learnings from theological learnings, reading the process of human self-disclosure from the vantage point of the divine self-disclosure, thinking through the therapeutic process from the perspective of its being illuminated by the emphatic love of God in Jesus Christ as the ontological basis for secular healing (pp. 124-125].

The proper use of analogy can and does provide guidelines for the human situation. This study is concerned with an investigation of marital analogy as found in the Scriptures. In the light of these findings, this study also shows how such an analogy provides guidelines for reconciliation in marriage.

The motivation for this study has developed from a personal desire to gain further insights regarding marital reconciliation under the instruction of Scripture. In addition to this personal desire, there was also the challenge presented for this study by Oden (1966) when he writes,

> What we do lack, however, is a constrained, careful use of analogy, deliberately conceived out of a clean self-consistent theological method and grounded in a serious doctrine of revelation. This has not been achieved and has hardly been attempted [p. 124].

CHAPTER II

OLD TESTAMENT MARITAL IMAGERY
Function of Analogy

By definition, any relationship between the Lord and His people is a relationship of love. The Old Testament uses numerous analogies to show the depth of God's love to His people. One analogy used by Old Testament writers is that of the marital relationship. The analogy of God as the husband and Israel as the wife provided the ancient Israelites with a clear conception of a heavenly reality with an earthly counterpart. This analogy provided guidelines for God's love to Israel and Israel's love to God.

The marital analogy encompasses both a divine relationship and a human relationship. In the Old Testament, Yahweh was considered to be the husband and Israel was described as the wife of Yahweh. By using this analogy, the Old Testament writers intended to show to Israel that Yahweh loved Israel as a husband loves his own wife. The analogy also provided a prototype for human marriage. The use of analogy can be seen in this instance as serving a dual function. It makes clear the divine relationship and also provides guidelines for the human relationship. In his book Analogy, Buchanan (1867) writes,

> Our religious and our relative duties resemble each other in this respect, that they depend on the relations which subsist, in the one case between man and man, in the other between man and God. These two sets of relations, when compared, are found to be analogous, in so much that common terms are applied to both: there is therefore much more than a superficial resemblance, there is an intimate and deep rooted analogy between the two.

Although the marital analogy provides guidelines for human marriage; it is recognized that the relationship between God and His people is not the same in all respects as the relationship of a husband and wife. God is the creator, the husband is His creation. God in His nature is perfect, the husband by nature is imperfect. God is God and the husband is man. In His Word, God speaks vividly of this difference, "I will not execute my fierce anger. I will not again destroy Ephraim; for I am God and not man [Hosea 11:9]." "For my thoughts are not your thoughts, neither are your ways my ways For as the heavens are higher than the earth, so are my ways higher than your ways, and my thoughts than your thoughts [Isaiah 55:8, 9]."

While this study acknowledges this difference, these two relationships (the Divine and the human) are intimately related in that they depend mutually upon one another. God used Israel's personal knowledge of the marital relation to illustrate His love. Without God's revelation of His love, Israel would not as fully know the meaning of human marriage. Buchanan (1867) speaks of this mutual dependency when he writes,

> It thus appears that Christian duty . . is analogous to natural duty, since both depend equally on certain relations which involve or imply moral obligation . . further, that our natural and revealed relations, although different, are also analogous to one another, so strictly analogous that the same ethical principles which are applicable to the former are applicable to the latter.

To this he adds,

> Suppose further that other relations between man and God . . are made known by the supernatural light of revelation, and that these again are analogous to certain other relations which are familiarly known—then the same duties which result from these relations as subsisting between man and man, result also from the same or similar relations as subsisting between man and God.

The use of analogy is a helpful tool In making theological and biblical truths apply to the everyday practical involvement in human affairs. It is at this point that the contemporary biblical theologians are meeting a major crisis. The crisis the church faces today is not understanding biblical theology, but in applying the truths of biblical theology to practical problems.

Of particular interest in this study is the application of biblical truths to the marital relation. Buchanan (1867) also writes of the usefulness of analogy, "We begin with the earthly and rise to heavenly things and thence descend again with a knowledge of truth which may be applied to practical use"

By using the marital imagery, the Old Testament writers enabled Israel to comprehend a concept beyond the borders of their minds. The marital imagery gave the Israelites a concrete message for understanding the personal encounter of God with His people. This in itself is the beauty of analogy as Farbridge (1923) writes, "The tendency to give a substantial visible form to an abstract idea is so deeply rooted in humanity, that it must be looked upon as responding to human necessity." Since a pictorial representation of an idea or a thought often produces a much better effect than a description in words, the prophets of Israel did not hesitate to use marital imagery as an attempt to express God's love toward Israel. This is the purpose of analogy, and Farbridge (1923) concurs when he writes, "Analogy is to represent but not reproduce a reality." Kahler (1960) views the importance of analogy when he writes, "All cultic symbols... are instituted acts of bridging distances between different existential spheres." He concludes that analogy "was meant to elucidate an abstraction by visualizing it, transferring it into an image [p. 72]." Tillich speaks more specifically regarding religious analogy when he writes, "Religious symbols are . . a representation of that which is unconditionally beyond the conceptual sphere, they point to the ultimate reality implied in the religious act, to what concerns us ultimately."

Marital Imagery in the Prophets

The first Old Testament prophet to employ the analogy of Yahweh as the husband of Israel was Hosea. Hosea began speaking of the marital imagery from a negative perspective, declaring that Yahweh was no longer, in a metaphorical sense, Israel's husband. He writes, "Plead with your mother [Israel], plead—for she is not my wife, and I am not her husband [Hosea 2:2]." Here Yahweh is represented as addressing the individual Israelites. The mother with whom they are to plead is the nation Israel as a whole. The fact Yahweh would say to Israel that she is no longer his wife is not merely a parenthetical phrase nor does it represent Yahweh as wholly abandoning Israel in the ultimate sense. This is rather a message which Hosea is asked to convey to Israel. The message is: (a) to declare a break in the marriage and (b) "to declare that Israel's 'whoredom' caused the break and brought shame and disgrace upon herself."

Ezekiel

The prophet Ezekiel recaptures the history of Israel in using bridal and marital imagery. In chapter sixteen, Ezekiel begins with a story about a baby who was left exposed after birth. She was found by a traveller who saved her life, and the child grew to be a fine looking young lady. The next time he passed her, she appeared beautiful to the traveller and he married her, and she became his queen. The story ends with a sad note, however, with the wife relying on her own beauty and becoming an unfaithful wife. The following verses are edited to give the major points of this story.

> Your origin and your birth are of the land of the Canaanites... on the day you were born, your navel string was not cut, nor were you washed with water... no eye pitied you... but you were cast out on the open field . on the day you were born. And when I passed by you I said to you in your blood, "Live and grow up like a plant of the field and you grew up and became tall and arrived at

full maidenhood; your breasts had formed and your hair had grown, yet you were naked and bare. When I passed you again and looked upon you, behold you were at the age for love... I plighted my troth to you and entered into covenant with you.. and you became mine. Then I bathed you with water and washed off your blood from you and anointed you with oil... I clothed you... and decked youwith ornaments... you ate fine flour and honey and oil. You grew exceedingly beautiful and came to regal estate... but you trusted in your beauty and played the harlot. You did not remember the days of your youth... How lovesick is your heart . seeing you did all these things the deeds of a brazen harlot [Ezekiel 16:1-30)!

In Ezekiel's use of analogy, the baby who became the king's wife was Israel. She was endowed with much love and many gifts, and still she proved to be unfaithful. Her licentiousness deserved the death penalty.

Israel trusted in her beauty and played the harlot. For Israel, Yahweh will make the punishment fit the crime. Batey (1971) speaks of this punishment when he writes that the Lord would deliver his unfaithful wife into the hands of her paramours in order that they might shame her (p. 8)

In punishing Israel, Yahweh displayed one aspect of the jealous love He held toward His wife. However, the jealous love also promised covenant renewal: "yet I will establish with you an everlasting covenant . and you shall know that I am the Lord. . when I forgive you all that you have done [Ezekiel 16:60-63]." The promise of covenant renewal was offered to Israel if she would turn with remorse from her waywardness.

Isaiah

Isaiah spoke of the marital imagery in comforting fashion which is typical of his writings:

> Fear not for you will not be ashamed... for you will forget the shame of your youth and the reproval of your womanhood you will remember no more. For your Maker is your Husband, the Lord of host is His name... for the Lord has called you like a wife forsaken and grieved in spirit, like a wife of youth she is cast off . For a brief moment I forsook you but with great compassion I will gather you. In overflowing wrath for a moment I hid my face from you, but with an everlasting love, I will have compassion on you [Isaiah 54:4-8].

Jeremiah

Jeremiah wrote of the marital imagery in regard to Israel's devotion and faithlessness. "I remember the devotion of your youth, your love as a bride, how you followed me in the wilderness in a land not sown [Jeremiah 2:1]." "Surely, as a faithless wife leaves her husband, so have you been faithless to me, O house of Israel [Jeremiah 3:20]."

Marital Imagery in Hosea

Many of the prophets wrote more extensively regarding the marital analogy between Yahweh and Israel than this study has indicated. In order to review the marital analogy more carefully, this study has selected the prophet Hosea as a central focus. It was Hosea who brought the essential nuptial character between Yahweh and Israel into Israel's consciousness. Because he was the first prophet to employ the use of marital imagery and due to the fact that he wrote from a personal experience of marital infidelity and reconciliation, the writings of Hosea are the object of further attention.

Background material

The roots of nuptial imagery were deep in the soil of Old Testament history. Yahweh initiated the marital relationship by choosing Israel for Himself. Yahweh spoke to Abraham with these words, "Go from your country and I will make you a great nation and I will bless you. I will bless those who bless you and him who curses you I will curse [Genesis 12:1-3]." Later the covenant was restated when Yahweh said to Abraham:

> Behold my covenant is with you, and you shall be the father of a multitude of nations... I will establish my covenant between me and you and your descendants after you throughout their generations for an everlasting covenant, to be God to you and your descendants after you [Genesis 17:4, 7].

Joseph, the great-grandson of Abraham, brought his family (Israel) to the land of Goshen in Egypt. Life in Goshen was good until the nationalistic spirit of the Egyptian pharaohs asserted itself with tremendous power and, consequently, matters took a turn for the worse for Israel. Moses writes regarding this period,

> Now there arose a new king over Egypt, who did not know Joseph. And he said to his people, "Behold, the people of Israel are too many and too mighty for us. Come let us deal shrewdly with them, lest they multiply... Therefore they set taskmasters over them to afflict them with heavy burdens [Exodus 1:8-11]

At the time of this great affliction, the people of Israel were soon to be released under the leadership of Moses. Following the great exodus from Egypt, Moses brought the people of Israel to the foot of Mount Sinai. In ceremonious fashion, the official consummation of the wedding between Yahweh and Israel took place. Chavasse (1939) writes, "For it is here that we find God choosing the chosen people binding them to Him in a covenant of protection and obedience." It was significant that prior to the ceremony of giving the law, Yahweh allowed Israel the freedom to choose partnership with Yahweh. The covenant made thereby was one of free choice and not one of coercion. The giving of the covenant at Sinai had an intimate relationship to the ratification of a marriage contract. Hanson (1946) writes,

> The Rabbis eulogized the conclusion of the covenant at Sinai as a marriage between Yahweh and His people. The Torah is the marriage contract, Moses is the one who leads the Bride and Yahweh meets Israel in the same way as the Bridegroom his Bride [p. 139].

Cobham (1951) writes, "The covenant was interpreted as a marriage covenant... Israel is the wife. Yahweh remains faithful to the marriage covenant and restores Israel to the original relationship."

Yahweh spoke to Moses and said,

> Thus... you shall tell the people of Israel, "you have seen what I did to the Egyptians and how I bore you on eagles wings and brought you to myself. Nowtherefore, if you will obey my voice and keep my covenant, you shall be mine own possession among all peoples" [Exodus 19:3-5].

The covenantal invitation of Yahweh and the acceptance of Israel was couched in marital language. In ancient Hebrew customs, the wife was considered the possession of the husband. After Israel accepted Yahweh's offer, Moses brought the people to meet Yahweh at Sinai where the two were married. Yahweh gave Moses specific instructions regarding the event of Israel coming to meet God.

> Go to the people and consecrate them today and tomorrow and let them wash their garments and be ready by the third day, for on the third day the Lord will come down upon Mount Sinai in the sight of all the people... When the trumpet sounds a long blast, they shall come up to the mountain. On the morning of the third day there were thunders and lightnings and thick cloud upon

the mountain and a very loud trumpet blast. Then Moses brought the people out of the camp to meet God [Exodus 19:10-17).

The prophets considered this event to be of significant worth. In their writings, the covenant at Sinai was frequently mentioned as an event to be recalled. Hosea called Israel to remember this significant event in their past history. The prophet called the people to remember that "I am the Lord your God from the land of Egypt; . . It was I who knew you in the wilderness, in the land of drought [Hosea 13:4, 5)." Batey (1971) says,

> For Hosea, the complex of preparatory events became focused at the Exodus, for here Yahweh dramatically revealed His choice and love for Israel . . With this historic act and the giving and the receiving of the covenant at Sinai, the Lord married His people. Israel had "honeymooned" with Yahweh in the desert wanderings [p. 4].

As the wife of Yahweh, Israel was soon granted entrance into the promised land under the leadership of Joshua. Once in the promised land of Canaan, she grew to "regal estate" with her glory reaching its height under the kingship of Solomon. Following the death of Solomon, the nation was disrupted. The united kingdom became the divided kingdom. The forces of internal decay and external pressure took their toll on Israel. During this period of deterioration, the nation Israel was described by Hosea as the unfaithful wife of Yahweh. Furthermore, her actions were compared to the actions of a "brazen harlot." It was at this time and place Hosea found his mission in the history of Israel.

Historical and cultural contingencies

Metaphorical terms used to describe the marital relationship have a rich and complex meaning. The meaning often reflects historical and cultural contingencies. Insofar that it is the endeavor of this study to understand the bridal imagery in the Christian Gospel, this chapter attempts to enter into the thought of the prophet Hosea in order to understand his point of view. The cultural context was intimately connected with Hosea's religious faith. This does not mean that the message of Hosea is unique from all other scriptural writers because of his unique time in history. It does mean that the book of Hosea focused itself upon the basic idea of Yahweh's people and His covenant with them. This theme runs through and holds together the varied literature of the Scriptures. Hosea wrote to a community which was conscious of itself as being, above all, the People of the Covenant. Hosea's use of bridal imagery was an attempt to speak of Israel's covenantal relationship with Yahweh. Therefore, the product of Hosea's pen was not merely some precise objective account of certain historical facts. Hosea's account was intended to reveal to Israel the saving grace of Yahweh. His account was written by an inspired preacher who was completely involved in the history he related. Because the New Testament church carne into being as a new Israel, it also inherited all the complexities of belief which accompanied the covenantal relationship. The New Covenant in Jesus Christ did not abolish the Old Covenant, but rather continued the central theme of the covenantal relationship between Yahweh and His chosen people. Hosea's book of prophecy was viewed as a fresh perspective, manifesting an old pattern of Yahweh's saving acts of election and redemption. Lampe (1957) claims that Hosea foresaw a repetition of the wilderness period where the significance of the covenant made at Sinai was brought to the attention of Israel.

> It is the pattern of divine action which the prophet discerns, rather than the recurrence of the outward historical events; but for him, as for Israelite thought as a whole, divine action is mediated in the actual events of history.

In connection with this, the message behind the bridal imagery must be understood as Hosea1s readers found this analogy meaningful to them. Greidanus (1970) supports this hermeneutical principle when he writes that,

A proper understanding of the text requires however that it be heard first of all as proclamation to the particular historical church to which it is specifically directed.

Jereboam II was king in Israel when Hosea began his prophetic office. Jereboam was the spokesman of the disgruntled majority and began his rule over the ten northern tribes of Israel following the death of King Solomon. Israel was experiencing a political and religious crisis. Politically, they lost their unity and strong centralized government. Religiously, they consolidated the worship of Yahweh with the Baal worship of the Canaanite culture. Israel was "religious 11 as they brought their sacrifices and offerings to the temples, but their worship was not from their hearts as evidenced by the poor, who were exploited and oppressed. Von Rad (1965) writes concerning the circumstances of Hosea's time,

> Only two basic data specific to the North need be mentioned; the disintegration of patriarchal Jahwism in the Canaanite fertility cult and the peculiar political and governmental system which existed there.

Following the death of Jereboam, Hosea openly assailed the kings and the people for their vile conduct. Israel's political anarchy and unrest weakened the country to such a degree that it was an easy conquest for the growing Assyrian enemy. He also sharply reprimanded the people for serving alien gods. The marital motif in this historical setting cannot be completely understood apart from Israel's encounter with the Canaanite fertility cult. Batey (1971) writes, "For primitive people the significance of a sacred marriage was bound up with the fertility of the land." Von Rad (1965) writes,

> Both Hosea and Ezekiel represent Yahweh as the spouse of mortal women without feeling any need to fear that these representations would be misunderstood as having mythical significance. On the other hand, in

these prophetic symbolizations are to be discerned as the demythologised survivals within Yahwehism of ideas derived from Canaan.

The Canaanites were sedentary people depending on an agrarian economy. Therefore, the fertility of the soil was of paramount importance with the Baal fertility cult, closely associated with the production of crops. The soil was not something indifferent, it was a holy thing and the creative powers were not a secular matter. Therefore, copulation rites with the deity safeguarded the work of tillage. Von Rad (1965) mentions the significance of the soil to the ancient mind when he writes, "The soil was not something indifferent; it was a holy thing, the rousing of whose powers was no secular matter... Curious rites therefore safeguarded the work of tillage.u Batey (1971) writes concerning the fertility of the soil,

> The Canaanites personified the various aspects of nature and projected this pantheon into a divine city state where gods vied for power and control. The Canaanites experienced in sex and fertility the secret of an abundant life. They transported the union of male and female to the mythic realm and saw in the fertile union of Baal and Anoth the release of power for fertility on earth.

The Baal worshippers believed that they did not encounter the deity directly. but rather it was through the magic of cultic acts prescribed by the Baal priest. "It was believed that the re-enactment of the mythological drama in the fertility ritual would stimulate the union of Baal and his consort, thereby producing fertility in the land [Batey, 1971].u Temple prostitutes were women of great cultic significance. Men visiting these women believed themselves to be partners for the forces of good. From this cultic form of worship came also the Canaanite concept of marriage. In the Canaanite marriage, the husband was conceived as the sower of the seed and the wife as the soil. The woman's body nurtured the seed as the soil nurtured the grain. Just as the plant grew from the seed, so the children grew from the man's seed.

In many respects, ancient Hebrew marriage was similar to the Canaanite concept of marriage. In the marriage, it was implied that men were superior to women. The relationship between husband and wife was similar to that of a possessor and his possession. The main duty of the wife was to obey her husband. If a wife committed adultery, she did the worst thing she could do to her husband. She allowed for the possibility of foreign seed in her womb or "soil," and thus endangered the integrity of mily line and violated her own marriage.

In ancient Israel, the fact that husbands were superior to their wives was a cultural given. Following the fall of Adam and Eve in the garden, Yahweh said to the woman that the husband shall rule over you (Genesis 3:16) Men were free to have more than one wife. They had the authority to divorce their wives. They were allowed to purchase their wives without mutual consent (Genesis 34: 11, 12; Deuteronomy 22:28, 29; 24:1-4). Thielicke (1964) writes, "The wife thereby passes into the power of the husband. Thus she has no part in this transaction as an independent individual under law." Wives were considered as the property of their husbands. A man would buy his wife as he would buy real estate or cattle. The Hebrew language supports this notion. The Hebrew word for man is clearly a reference to the husband as the owner or the possessor of his wife. The Hebrew word for wife means soft and delicate. This word, in its proper context, is translated as "wifeu with the connotation of being a possession of her husband.

Biblical data describing the ancient Hebrew marriage reveal similarities of Canaanite marriages to Israelite family life. However, to say this and nothing more regarding Hebrew marriage would hardly do justice to the marital institution as the Hebrews understood marriage in the light of Yahweh's commands. Underlying the apparent Canaanite resemblance of marital life, there was a deep and abiding love relationship between husband and wife. Marriage was regarded not as a convenient social contract between a man and a woman, but a divine ordinance. At a different level, the Hebrews judged that it was not good for a man to be without a wife. In connection with the joys of marriage, Proverbs declares that a man ought to "rejoice in the wife of your youth . Let her affection fill you at all times with delight, be infatuated always with her love [Proverbs 5:18, 19]." Moore (1946) speaks of this abiding relation when he writes, "One who has no wife remains without good, and without a helper, and without joy, and without a blessing and without atonement." There is little indication in the Old Testament narrative that either the husband or the wife objected to this particular form of marriage. Thus, the biblical concept of the woman did not conceive of her as an inferior being, but as an equal partner of her husband and a person in her own right. There was a personal sense of belonging to one another. Love between husbands and wives transcended the necessary legal transactions. W. G. Cole, in his book Sex and Love in the Bible writes,

> There was however a high value placed upon wifehood and motherhood, as the laws against adultery, harlotry and rape clearly show. The Decalogue placed mother on an equal plane with father in the command enjoining filial honor and obedience.

From this political, religious, and social setting, Israel, as Yahweh's wife, was entangled in an unending struggle between their obedience to Yahweh and their encounter with Canaanite practices. R. A. Batey, in his book New Testament Studies, writes,

> The infiltration of the nomadic Israelites into the agrarian Canaanite region precipitated a struggle between divergent religious and cultural forces. The conflict created degrees of reaction... Some Israelites apostacized completely from Yahweh and "went a whoring after Baal." Other Israelites... excluded themselves from agriculture (Jeremiah 35:1-19). However, it was between these extremes that the heat of the battle, Yahweh versus Baal, was to be fought.

Hosea the prophet conveyed the message of Yahweh through a symbolic metaphor. It was his purpose to stress and underscore the truth of his prophecy and to warn the people of the consequences they would have to face if they should still refuse to heed his words. In order for Hosea to make an impact on Israel, he made astonishing use of the marital metaphor in which he depicted Yahweh being married to his people. In his commentary on Hosea, J.M. Ward writes that Hosea was taking a risk in having the marital metaphor misunderstood but adds that Hosea's use of the metaphor was not an accommodation to the worship of fertility gods. It was part of his polemic against it. He described the "divine wife"... as a mundane prostitute and, in doing so, he negated the baalistic theology and emptied it of its power... it is hard to imagine a more powerful or memorable one.

Hosea's message was focused in Yahweh's dramatic love toward Israel in calling the people to remember the wonderful history of Yahweh who graciously took His people out of Egypt. By alluding to Israel's history, he made a striking contrast with her present condition. Israel forsook Yahweh like an adulterous wife fleeing from her husband for other lovers. By declaring Israel an adulterous wife within the marital analogy, Hosea made a double impact on his audience. In Israel, any woman found guilty of adultery was worthy of capital punishment which was death by stoning (Deuteronomy 22:23-27). Adultery consisted of a betrothed woman willingly engaging in sexual intercourse with someone other than her betrothed husband. Secondly, the central thrust of Hosea's message came from his own personal marriage tragedy with a wife who proved to be faithless. From Hosea's intense personal knowledge, he powerfully illustrated the relationship between Yahweh and Israel. Batey meaningfully describes the relationship,

> Israel's faithlessness... like Gomer, was transient. "Like a morning cloud, like dew that goes early away" her love vanished. Hosea depicted Israel as playing the harlot... with vivid metaphor. Hosea envisioned the nation as an oestrous heifer solicitous of the Baal bull (Hosea 4:16)

Adultery within the Marital Imagery Hosea 2:2, 4:1-2, 5:4)

The marital relation between Yahweh and Israel was clearly in need of renewal. Yahweh was represented as speaking with the prophet saying, "Plead with your mother, plead—for she is not my wife, and I am not her husband [Hosea 2:2]." This passage is surrounded by the marriage of Hosea and Gomer which is a plain symbol of the marriage of Yahweh and Israel. W.R. Harper writes, "The sense of the symbol is plain: (1) the prophet represents Yahweh; (2) Gomer who is married to the prophet is Israel who is married to Yahweh." He also adds, "as Gomer after marriage goes astray, so Israel, after a period goes a whoring after other gods."

Israel's disobedience was compared to that of an adulterous woman. The Hebrew word for adultery implies adultery on behalf of the wife with a man other than her husband. In this context, the word implies adultery on behalf of the wife with a man other than her husband). In the marriage between Yahweh and Israel, the party responsible for the bifurcation was Israel's disobedience and faithlessness.

Chapter four of Hosea speaks more explicitly regarding this broken relation:

Hear the word of the Lord O Israel; for the Lord has a controversy with the inhabitants of the land. There is no faithfulness or kindness, and no knowledge of God in the land; there is swearing, lying, killing, stealing, and committing adultery; they break all bounds and murder follows murder [Hosea 4:1-2].

In these verses, the prophet speaks of the contention Yahweh had with his wife, Israel, with Yahweh placing directly before her the formal charges against his wife. Harper observes that this was a quarrel within the relationship and Israel failed to observe the terms of this relationship. He writes, "This was not merely 'a just cause', nor a reproof, accusation, but a contention, quarrel. A relationship has existed between Yahweh and Israel, the terms of which Israel has not observed."

These charges were first stated as sins of omission. The sins of commission follow as a logical result of the spiritual void found in verse one. The Hebrew word for "no faithfulness" is a feminine noun. It also means, to confirm and support." This Hebrew word also means firmness, faithfulness, and truth." The first formal charge against Israel was that she was no longer faithful or truthful. Harper adds, "By truth he means fidelity, honesty, constancy, trustworthiness in thought, word, and deed." In addition, there was no kindness. The Hebrew word used by Hosea specifically refers to kindness shown to the lowly, needy, and those in need of compassionate love.

D.A. Hubbard, in his book, With Bands of Love, writes that there are sins of oppression which the prophets so frequently berate: foreclosing on widows (Micah 2:9), oppression of the poor (Micah 2:2), the greediness of the rich (Amos 2:6), the failure to return pledge garments (Amos 2:8), the travesties of justice which the rich perpetrated against the poor in law courts (Micah 7:3), the general selfishness and greed (Micah 3:1-3).

Finally, we read that there was no knowledge of God in the land. The Hebrew word for "no knowledge" means "no knowledge no knowledge of God in the highest sense". This also includes no obedience. Finally, this Hebrew word was very frequently used by the Hebrews as a particle of negation. In this case, Hosea used this Hebrew word to emphasize the utter lack and the nonexistence of obedience, compassion, and kindness. D.A Hubbard rightfully notes, "The entire spiritual defection of Israel may be accounted for on the basis of this one fact: they did not know the Lord." Israel's sin was disobedience which manifested itself in direct violation to the law given at Mount Sinai upon which they had agreed to keep as part of the contractual agreement of the marital vows. Dr. Hubbard continues, "The theme of. . disobedience dominates the context here. The three great lacks and the catalog of sins which follows point to a basic attitude of disobedience to the revealed law of God."

Dr. Ward specifically describes Israel's disobedience:

> The three great crimes of murder, robbery, and adultery appear to have constituted an especially memorable and significant triplicity, not only among prophetic and priestly circles, but also among the sages of Israel.

Hosea Chapter five measured the intensity of her disobedience. "Their deeds do not permit them to return to their God. For the spirit of harlotry is within them, and they know not the Lord [Hosea 5:4]." Yahweh, through His prophets, continually called the Israelites to obedience and, therefore, Israel could not excuse herself. Israel displayed in her life a willful obstinancy that even the prophets were not able to bend her away from her stubbornness. Consequently, they were not able to return to Yahweh on their own accord. John Calvin writes that the wife of Yahweh was

> "Soul pleased" with her own filthiness, that there is no shame, no fear . . the Israelites are so imbued with their superstitions, that they cannot be restored to the right way on their own.

<u>Reconciliation within Marital Imagery</u>

As Israel's disobedience and covenant-breaking was clearly stated, so also was the process of reconciliation. Although a prophet of doom, Hosea was also a prophet of hope. Dr. Batey introduces Hosea's message of hope by stating, Hosea looked beyond the dark clouds of impending tribulation to a future which took seriously not only Israel's faithfulness, but also God's faithfulness. The Lord will bring her once more to the wilderness, where he had first known her, he will speak to her heart. He who knew her in the wilderness not only will be recognized but acknowledged as "my Husband".

Israel's restoration was promised in Hosea 2:16-20.

Within the process of reconciliation, Yahweh, the husband, took the initiative to sustain the covenant bond with His people. In the perspective of viewing God as the Redeemer of Israel, Dr. N.H Snaith, in his book Amos, Hosea, and Micah, writes, "The righteousness of God shows itself in His saving work the emphasis is on God's mighty work in saving the humble, those devoted ones who trust in Him."

In connection with this, Dr. H.W Robinson writes of God's initiative action:

> In the first place, Israel has grasped the essential truth for all religion, that in the fellowship of God and man, God must be active as well as man. Yahweh of Israel, in definite and unmistakable ways, comes out to meet man and does not simply wait for man's approach.

At another point in his book, Robinson becomes more specific when he writes, "Yahweh has taken the initiative by sending his prophets."

Another aspect of Yahweh's initiative was the expression of His anger and judgment upon Israel for their covenant-breaking. The anger and judgment of Yahweh is revealed only after He continuously pleads with Israel to repent. His anger is revealed against Israel only as a last resort for her repeated failure to heed the warnings of the prophets. The marital metaphor does contain within itself an emphasis on the jealous love of Yahweh as a rejected husband, who demands faithfulness to the covenant (Hosea 4:5; 5:15; 7:2, 4; 8:5; 9:12, 15; 13:9).

Dr. Batey writes of Yahweh's love, "Therefore the metaphor, also has the capacity to express alienation, wrath and judgment; but because Israel is the wife of Yahweh there is implicitly the element of hope as well."

In view of Yahweh's jealous love, expressed by His anger, Yahweh also spoke the words of forgiveness and covenant renewal. Through the promise of reconciliation and covenant renewal, Yahweh was determined to create a people faithful to Himself. Hosea spoke of this restoration when he wrote,

And in that day, says the Lord, you will call me "my husband" and no longer will you call me "my Baal". For I will remove the names of the Baals from her mouth and they shall be mentioned by name no more. And I will make for you a covenant on that day with the beast of the field, the birds of the air, and the creeping things of the ground; and I will abolish the bow, the sword and war from the land; and I will make you lie down in safety. And I will betroth you to me forever; I will betroth you to me in righteousness and in justice, in steadfast love and in mercy. I will betroth you to me in faithfulness and you shall know the Lord [Hosea 2: 16-20].

The prophet spoke of a new marriage which envisioned the adulterous wife to enter into marriage as a pure bride once again. Yahweh promised to renew the marriage covenant in which her former sins would be of no consequence to the marital relation. John Calvin speaks of this marital renewal when he writes,

... for God thereby means that he would not remember the unfaithfulness for which he had before cast away his people, but would blot out all their infamy. It was indeed an honorable reception into favour, when God offered a new marriage, as though the people had not been like an adulterous woman.

Hosea appears to emphasize the bond of loving-kindness which united Yahweh to His people. His personal experience of a faithless wife whom he still loved opened his eyes to a deeper meaning of the bond between Yahweh and his people. His idea of Yahweh interpreted through the deepest relationship of life enabled Hosea to write about the passionate love of Yahweh for His bride. Rowley views the agonizing personal experience of Hosea as an occasion for an intense awareness of the depth of God's love.

...the wife whom Hosea deeply loved was unfaithful to him and... her infidelity brought him intense anguish yet without destroying his love, so that he found God approaching him through his agony to illumine his mind with an understanding of the depth of the divine love for Israel that is unsurpassed in the Old Testament.

In the light of this, he witnesses the nation Israel perishing because they do not know The Lord. The word Hosea uses to describe this aspect of God's love for his wife was ttSteadfast Loveu. Hosea's own domestic experience taught him what the Lord's love means. Because of his own attitude to his wayward wife, he came to know the love of God is steadfast and determined. No matter what Israel did on her part, Hosea understood God's underlying love for Israel and His unwillingness to completely abandon her. Snaith (1950) perceives Hosea making this idea abundantly clear in his use of bridal imagery. He writes,

But through all the troubles which beat against and broke the marriage covenant between Jehovah and Israel, there was one fact which never changed. This was God's sure love for Israel. Because of this unswerving love, the Covenant can never be finally and completely broken. It takes two to make a covenant and it also takes two to break it. Israel may have rejected God, but God has not rejected Israel.

In the face of God's steadfast love, The Lord provides a door of hope by promising a new covenant whereby God will "betroth" Israel to himself forever. In addition to God's Steadfast Love, the next step in the process of Reconciliation is to show a real effort to make a complete break from all past irresponsible and wrong behavior.

The Lord wants a clean cut with the past and there will be a new Covenant. Now the Lord says that he will "betroth" Israel forever. A betrothal is a sacred relationship in which the husband pays a high price as a gift to his bride This gift is a means by which the act of betrothal is accomplished. The Lord betrothed Israel with the gift of righteousness, justice, mercy, and faithfulness. Once this gift is received, restoration is complete. The phrase "you shall know the Lord," marks the climax of The betrothal. This promise was made by Jesus Christ when he betrothed himself to his bride the Church.

Repentance and Confession in Marital Imagery (Hosea 5:15-6:1)

The process of marital reconciliation between The Lord and Israel contains both God's divine initiative and human responsibility. The Lord, by His own good will, extends His hand to Israel in spite of her faithlessness and disobedience. However, in every covenant, there are two parts. The process of reconciliation also includes responsibilities placed upon Israel, the wife. Broadly speaking, the responsibilities placed upon Israel require both confession of her sin in genuine repentance. The second aspect of covenant renewal involved the need for Israel to acknowledge her guilt and return to the Lord. God says He will not return to Israel,

> "...until they acknowledge their guilt and seek my face,
> and in their distress, they seek me saying, "Come, let us
> return to the Lord; for He has torn, that He may heal us;
> He has stricken, and He will bind us up [Hosea 5:15-6:1]."

The period of The Lord's withdrawal and separation from Israel was no doubt most agonizing. Nevertheless, the prophet Hosea continually warned Israel against their departure from The Lord's commands and against their repetitive refusal to repent. The prophet spoke of The Lord's vengeance and how God would abandon Israel until she turned to acknowledge her husband and repent. The Lord's departure is to be understood from the perspective of Israel. Calvin (1950), in his commentary of Hosea, speaks to this point of The Lord's turning away from Israel,

> "God here declares that after having been dreadfully
> fierce against both the kingdoms of Judah and Israel, he
> would for a time rest quietly and wait from heaven what

they would do. This mode of thinking seems apparently strange when God says that he will go away; for he neither so hides himself in heaven, that he neglects human affairs, nor withdraws his hand... nor even takes away his spirit from men, especially when he would lead them to repentance.

Historically, the Lord did in fact turn away from Israel. This was the time of Israel's exile. During this period of captivity, The Lord could not be found until Israel cried out to Him from a genuinely penitent heart. This form of punishment for Israel was not intended to satisfy God's wrath but rather to promote Israel's salvation and bring her once again into the marital relationship. The goal and purpose of The Lord's abandonment was always restoration. When Israel acknowledges their sin, reconciliation begins within the metaphorical marital relationship.

Calvin understood the word "acknowledged to mean "confession. He writes,

> "But now the prophet distinctly shows that it is to seek God, when people acknowledge and confess their sins... So also in this place he says, "Until they confess that they have sinned, I will for a time hide myself".

When the Israelites would confess their iniquities, God at once would turn and have mercy on them. In Hebrew law, the obligation to confess sin is plain. The book of Numbers makes this clear, "When a man or woman commits any of the sins that breaks faith with the Lord, they shall confess their sin and make full restitution for their wrong [Numbers 5: 6],

In Proverbs, we read, "He who conceals his transgressions will not prosper, but he who confesses and forsakes them will obtain mercy [Proverbs 28: 13]." Again, Hosea writes, nReturn, 0 Israel, to the

Lord your God, Take with your words and return to the Lord [Hosea 14:1,2] .n Richardson (1951) speaks of the word, "to return" in marital terminology,

> "In the Old Testament the idea of repentance is often expressed by such words as "turn," "return." The fundamental idea behind the use of these words in a religious sense is that of . . a faithless wife returning to her husband. It represents a re-orientation of one's whole life and personality, which includes the adoption of a new ethical line of conduct, a forsaking of sin and turning to righteousness.

The marital breakdown with The Lord and Israel is not final! The way of reconciliation was open to a new experience of love in penitence and confession which would lead to a new union between those who were once husband and wife. Repentance was necessary in restoring the broken relationship.

Calvin (1950) views this as the beginning step in the process of reconciliation when he writes, "The first step of healing... is to be touched with grief... afterward to add this second thing—to seek the face of God, that is to present himself a suppliant before God and to ask for pardon.

> "Repentance begins in thought and its effect is instantaneous. But it is further followed up by words of confession... Repentance means that the sinner... must also confess with his lips and give expression to the thoughts which he determined in his heart. The regret includes the feeling of shame."

A second aspect of repentance involves a resolve not to commit the sin again. This also means living in faithfulness to the covenant pledge. If a person repented and went back to their sins, that was hardly a genuine restoration. However, genuine restoration is a person's determination to break away from their sins which were confessed. Therefore, confession is not a guarantee against a relapse into the former habits of their sins.

Throughout the history of Israel and especially at the period of their decline, the central theme of the prophets was The Lord's priceless gift of grace. God was willing and ready to offer Israel all the benefits of being his wife where she would truly "know" The Lord in the most intimate and personal manner. The Lord made one demand upon his wife. The demand was for Israel to face the truth about herself by way of repentance, confession, and restitution. This was the way of marital reconciliation between God and His wife Israel.

D. S. Bailey (1952) summarizes the essence of marital Reconciliation. He writes,

> Breakdown and even divorce, however, need not be final; they need not mean permanent separation. Penitence, reconciliation and a new experience of love can lead to the emergence of a new "one flesh" union between those who were once husband and wife and who, through the sin and pain of relational failure, have been brought by the spirit to a new mind and a desire to atone for the past. But when this happens, it does not mean that the new relation has been resuscitated; that is impossible, for the love which was once between them has been destroyed and can never be revived. Rather a new love has been born out of penitence and forgiveness; they have entered into a new relation, entirely distinct from the old, yet conditioned forever by a purged recollection of the failure which has been redeemed.

In conclusion, the marital image in Hosea is all we need to know about reconciliation between ourselves and God. The marital imagery also provides us with everything we need to understand reconciliation between a husband and wife. The first principle in marriage is:

"Choose wisely". Hosea did not choose wisely. Nevertheless, God commanded him to marry a prostitute. Her name was Gomer. This marriage was intentional for God to speak of His desire to reconcile with Israel. I do not believe that it is ever in God's plan for human marriage for a man to marry a prostitute. The first principle of "choosing wisely" is a broad topic, probably a topic for another book. My grandma Effie (my mother's mother) said to me when I was in high school, and I quote, "Eric, marry your own kind". Grandma Effie did not have a prejudicial bone in her body, but her statement holds a great deal of wisdom—what she was intending to say was, marry a person who loves the Lord. Marry a person that you have many things in common. Marry a person that you deeply love and are compatible. Marry a person that you can live with for the rest of your life. And finally, I think the best part of marriage and choosing wisely is to choose Jesus Christ as your Lord, savior, and master.

I think the second principle in marriage is that neither the husband or the wife are perfect. We all have and will violate the vows that we made on our wedding day. Some to greater degrees, and some to lesser degrees.

I believe that the third principle of marriage is when a vow is broken, acknowledge it quickly. Take responsibility for your own behavior and wrongdoing. Don't hide it or conceal it or continue in unlawful or wrong behavior.

The fourth principle is, always come to Jesus and confess your wrongdoing. When appropriate, share your wrong behavior with your spouse. I think it's important to express to one another the exact nature of your sin.

Principle number five is to make restitution by yourself. Restitution means that you have to put back what you have stolen. Do your best to never continue in wrong behavior.

Principle number six, the last principle for reconciliation and marriage: always show love, compassion, and kindness. In the Old Testament, it has already been clearly shown the wrath and anger of God against breaking covenantal promises. But as angry as God was towards Israel (God's wife), The Lord loved Israel with an eternal love. He promised redemption and restoration in Jesus Christ. One of my favorite passages in the bible is from the psalm of Solomon. God speaks to Israel with such kind words: "My dove, hiding in the cleft of the rock, come out and show me your face, and let me hear your voice, for your face is beautiful and your voice is sweet." Why is the dove hiding in the cleft of the rock? Possibly shame. Possibly guilt. Possibly involved with bad behavior and wrongdoing. No matter what the negative behavior might be, God seeks out the sinner and wants his wife to come forth for a new and better relationship. God is good all the time, God is good! Before I begin Chapter III, which is the Pauline Marital Imagery, I am going to take a brief intermission. This intermission will cover the entire word of God from beginning to end. Please bear with me as it will be very short. In Genesis, we read, "In the beginning, God created the heavens and the Earth." He created the man in his own image.

But God realized the man was lonely, and he created a woman. And then God said, you can have a good life if you follow my commandments. The only commandment—God gave was to not eat of the fruit of the tree of the knowledge of good and evil. Well, that didn't work out too good. They both disobeyed God, and they were aware of their shame and nakedness.

Nevertheless, in God's great love and compassion, he provided a way out. God said that he will send his son Jesus to restore all things. God said that Jesus will crush the head of the serpent who tempted our happy couple, and he said that Satan would only bruise the heel of the deliverer, Jesus.

Things went along pretty well, until God called Abraham to be his chosen people. This was the nation of Israel. But that didn't work out too good either. Soon, Israel became slaves and in bondage to the pharaohs of Egypt. While in captivity, God rescued and raised up Moses. Moses led the people out of Egypt and saved the chosen ones who put blood of lambs on the door post. This was called the Passover. When the Angel of Death saw the blood, they passed over the household and all were saved from the plague of death. Moses led the people through the Red Sea, and into a barren wilderness.

But that didn't work out too good either. The people complained bitterly. So, God called Moses to Mount Sinai with the intent to marry the people of Israel. The marriage was both the giving and receiving of sacred vows. God gave Israel the Ten Commandments and said, "If you keep these commandments, I will bless you." When Moses came down from the mountain for the marriage ceremony, he became very angry and broke the Ten Commandments to pieces because the Israelites made a golden calf and worshipped a dead idol. So the first marriage did not work out so good either. God called Moses to Sinai the second time, and when he came down from the mountain with the Ten Commandments, God ordered the people to come forth to the foot of the mountain. He ordered the people to cleanse themselves and come in white robes. This time the marriage ceremony worked, and they put the Ten Commandments in a traveling tabernacle. But as time went on, this marriage didn't work out so good either, and Israel became a very wicked, stiff necked, stubborn people who refused to keep the marriage agreement (the covenant). This marriage didn't work out so good either, and God wrote Israel a bill of divorce. Nevertheless, in His great mercy and compassion, he promised a new covenant. This new covenant was the birth of Jesus Christ, who was born of the Virgin Mary. Jesus became the perfect Lamb of God that took away the sins of the world. Now, from the marriage imagery, we have the betrothal imagery of Jesus being the bridegroom and the church as his bride. I believe that the suffering and the death and resurrection of Jesus Christ met all the requirements for atonement and a new marriage. As I will point out in the next chapter, the crucifixion of Christ was the high nuptials for the new wedding that God promised. Jesus rose from the grave, ascended into heaven, and will come again to receive his glorious bride, and then there will be a great wedding ceremony and a great wedding feast in heaven for all those who confess to be the glorious bride of Christ. Finally, at Jesus coming again, things will work out perfectly.

CHAPTER III

PAULINE MARITAL IMAGERY
Old Testament Marital Imagery—Transformation

When Israel returned to Palestine from Babylonian captivity, her religious life had changed from what it had been before her destruction. Her captivity proved to have a humbling effect. Now free from captivity, she was willing to listen to the Word of the Lord. There was an unparalleled religious "revival" led by the leaders of Israel. Israel was once again called to repent of her sins and return unto her God (Ezra, Nehemiah). This time the prophets found a receptive people. The prophets found a willing audience which heeded their words, something that would hardly have happened during all the years of Israel's former independence. Released from captivity with her renewed spirit and her renewed consciousness of God's love, Israel's single aim was to build and strengthen herself as a nation once again.

During the intertestamental period, Israel experienced new political struggles. Throughout this period, there was a struggle to control Palestine which was situated at the eastern end of the Mediterranean Sea, and it was a buffer state between the powers of the North, East, and South. Palestine was the principal arena for military operations. Only the rise of a new and greater power could have brought peace to this unstable region.

Such a power was Rome and its occupation of Palestine produced significant changes in the life of Israel. Israel once again saw herself as being under the power of another nation. From her religious and political struggle with Rome, there emerged a transformation in the biblical bridal imagery. The transformation in Old Testament marital imagery finds expression in first century B.C. Jewish apocalyptic thought which looked forward to a divine Messiah. Batey (1971) writes,

Under the influence of apocalyptic thought, which flourished in first century Judaism, a significant transformation of the prophetic marriage figure occurred. The Jewish people were no longer considered to have been married to Yahweh in the past, i.e., at Sinai. Disillusionment and pessimism regarding earthly existence prompted the apocalyptists to look longingly into the future for some decisive divine deliverance. This anticipation of a future age of messianic bliss made it difficult to take seriously the idea that Israel was married to the Holy One in her immediate historical condition. The prophetic metaphor was consequently modified with the Bride figure rather than the wife figure. Israel must wait until the messianic day when that which she possessed through promise would become hers in reality at the messianic marriage. It is this development of nuptial imagery which exemplifies the strongest affinity to the N.T. figure of the Church as the Bride of Christ.

The new belief advanced by the Jewish people embodied the hope of a coming Messiah who would save Israel. Cahn (1962) writes,

> The time of the greatest national catastrophe in Jewish history gave birth to the hope for eventual redemption. The Messianic idea is the belief that a scion of the house of David will redeem the Jewish people from exile. The Jews will then return to the land of Israel, the temple will be rebuilt, and a Jewish king will once again sit upon the throne in Jerusalem.

Even in the face of Israel's return to Palestine following the Babylonian captivity, the union of the two former kingdoms—Judah and Israel—with a king from the house of David never came to pass. Since this hope was never realized, widespread despondency prevailed among the Jewish people. Batey writes,

> The unfulfilled dream of the Jewish people in the face of Roman occupation gave rise to an even stronger hope

for national independence and restoration. The figure of Israel as a bride awaiting a future marriage with the Messiah provided an adequate expression for national aspirations.

The idea of the Messiah as the bridegroom coming to receive his bride found its way into the writings of St.Paul. Paul's use of bridal imagery has its source in his integration of Old Testament marital imagery, the apocalyptic hope for a coming Messiah, and Paul's knowledge of the teachings and the life of Jesus Christ. Central to this study are three passages in which Paul uses bridal imagery. These passages are: II Corinthians 11:1-3, Romans 7:1-6, and Ephesians 5:21-33.

Pauline Betrothal Imagery–II Corinthians 11:1-3

In the Pauline Corpus, the first documented use of bridal imagery is II Corinthians 11:1, 2, and 3. Paul writes,

> I wish you would bear with me in a little foolishness. Do bear with me. I feel a divine jealousy for you for I betrothed you to Christ to present you as a pure bride to her one husband. But I am afraid that as the Serpent deceived Eve by his cunning, your thoughts will be led astray from a sincere and pure devotion to Christ.

Church's opponents aroused Paul's jealousy

With Paul's use of betrothal imagery, it might appear that he is introducing a new thought. However, Paul 15 continuing to make a defense against the attacks made on him by his opponents which is in keeping with the context of the surrounding verses. Paul begins this chapter in protecting himself against the charges of "vanity" and "self praise" made by his opponents.

When Paul writes, "Bear with me in a little foolishness (II Corinthians 11:1) These words are not intended to mean that the subject material which follows is "foolishness." Rather, Paul casually dismisses the charges put against him. His opponents apparently had accused him of being jealous for the Corinthian church.

Paul's foes were vicious and subtle. They attacked his character, his gospel, and his personal life. The church at Corinth had allowed a band of Greek-speaking Jews to promote their teachings. These teachers were allowed entrance to the Corinthian church as they came declaring themselves missionaries, teachers of righteousness, with Apostolic commendation from the church of Jerusalem. These teachers insisted on the Law. They claimed that Paul ignored it and declared it obsolete. They declared that they were ministers of Christ and that Paul was not (II Corinthians 11:23).

> Saint Paul's opponents were trying to prove that he was no true apostle, and that as a preacher he was miserably ineffective. They bitterly assailed his private character. They said he was altogether, a despicable person, he never knew his own mind, he was a tyrant, and... he was a coward.

In addition, Paul's opponents stated that they were the genuine and authentic church leaders, taking credit for the church at Corinth.

> In addition, Paul's opponents professed to have a great zeal for religion. They did not mingle with heathen people. Paul is harsh and called them "Satan's Ministers" (II Corinthians 10: 15, 16; II Corinthians 11: 15)

So, it was in this context that Paul writes, "I feel a divine jealousy for you". Paul was in acute danger but his jealousy for the church of Corinth was a God-given jealousy. In this case a justified concern for the honor and purity of the Church at Corinth Paul's jealousy over the Corinthian church is not merely a human jealousy of selfish possessiveness. No, Paul's jealousy matches the divine jealousy of God for Israel in the Old Testament. The Lord said, "I am a jealous God".

This is a jealousy which is right and is the safeguard of love. It comes into play when those who love God are in danger from people who want to corrupt their minds or their characters. It right to say that this is a real fear which is at the root of damage to the church and the bride of Christ.

In the Old Testament, God uses the analogy of Him being the "husband" who is jealous in regard to his "wife" Israel. When Paul therefore associates the jealousy with himself... he is referring back to this Old Testament imagery.

Paul's jealousy for the Corinthian church is in the background for his use of betrothal imagery. By using betrothal imagery, he creates a tension between the prophetic warnings and the Lord's endorsement to faithfulness. Paul's use of betrothal imagery was a concept which the people of his time readily comprehended. In New Testament times, it was often customary for a woman's father to arrange the betrothal. By using this betrothal custom, Paul betrothed the Corinthian church to Christ. He presented the church to Christ as His bride (Revelation 21:2, 9; 22:17). The ancient custom of betrothal was much different from present-day understanding of the engagement period. The nature of Rabbinic Law regarding betrothal was not a mere promise to marry but it was the very initiation of marriage. The betrothal parties were regarded as married, though not yet entitled to all the marital rights. Also, the betrothed couple were not bound to fulfill any of the mutual duties of conjugal life. Sexual conjugal rights were not allowed until the marriage was made official. Faithlessness on the part of the female was considered adultery.

Paul uses this imagery to clarify the interactions between God, Christ, the Corinthian church, and himself. Paul understood his role as the father who arranged the betrothal and guards jealously over his daughter's faithfulness and purity. In ancient Israel, it was the father's right to give his daughter in marriage to an approved bridegroom.

Likewise, God, the spiritual father has given the church to be betrothed to an approved bridegroom. This approved bridegroom is none other than Jesus Christ. The use of Paul's betrothal imagery is a solid ground for the Divine marital union between Christ and his Church, the bride.

Prophetic warning as an expression of divine jealousy

Now Paul gives a prophetic warning to the church. He says that false teachers are like the "Serpent", who promised enlightenment as the reward of disloyalty and disobedience. Therefore, compromising loyalty to Christ would violate the Corinthians' status as a pure bride. As an expression of Paul's divine jealousy, Paul now compares himself as the father of the bride who continually warns her and watches over her purity, much like the Old Testament prophets repeatedly warned Israel against consorting with false gods.

Paul's encouragement to the Corinthian church may be viewed as the positive side of divine jealousy. Paul's use of bridal imagery has the capacity to express the theme of the believer's faithful response to the faithfulness of God's elective love in Jesus Christ. In stressing the theme of faithfulness, Paul reminded the Corinthian church of their betrothal to Jesus Christ as a past fact in history.

Therefore, Paul encourages the church to be faithful to her Lord. He stresses the fidelity in the marital relation since he senses the dangers of false teachings.

Paul's concern for the marriage of the church to Christ is of special interest since he was the person who arranged the betrothal. Paul's interest in the marriage of the church and Christ is his utmost passion. Paul was jealous and anxious that nothing should interfere with this marriage. The betrothed woman must devote herself exclusively to her destined Husband and must not allow her thoughts to be diverted to any other temptations. This is why Paul was so harsh on those who were distracting the Corinthian Church from their loyalty to Christ.

Paul's use of betrothal imagery made it possible to understand how the church found its purpose in both the realization and the anticipation of being the wife of Christ. Paul believed that the church experienced the presence of her Lord. He believed that the church in her present historical situation was indeed the bride of Christ. At the same time, the church also looked forward to the day when the wedding would consummate their relationship. Even though the church experienced the presence of her Lord, she still hoped for a future consummation. Such a relationship found expression in Paul's use of betrothal imagery. There is a time the church experiences between her acceptance in faith of Jesus Christ and her final consummation with Christ at His second coming. This 'time between' is not only a time for preparation but an opportunity to sustain devotion to Jesus Christ.

Paul's encouragement to the church to be faithful was the counterpoint to Paul's prophetic warning to the church against those who would seduce the church away from her one husband. In this connection, Paul's use of betrothal imagery shares a basic perspective with apocalyptic Jewish thought which was a modification of Old Testament marital imagery in which Israel was encouraged to be the faithful wife of Yahweh.

Betrothal imagery, as found in Paul's writing, integrates both the idea of faithfulness represented in Old Testament covenantal relationship and the idea of living in faithful obedience until the coming day of the Lord as represented in apocalyptic Jewish thought.

Hughes (1962) sees Paul making use of this bridal imagery as being closely related to Old Testament bridal imagery when he writes,

> In the apostle's language here we may discover further evidence of the identification of Christ in the New Testament with Jehovah in the Old Testament. It belongs to the essence of Apostolic Christology that Christ, who is the husband of God's people under the new dispensation, is none other than Jehovah, who is the husband of his

people under the former dispensation and therefore is the ever living bridegroom of those who are his .. The inference is clear also that the church of the N.T. which is the bride of Christ, is continuous with the church of the O.T. which is the bride of Jehovah. Hence Paul elsewhere describes the church as the "Israel of God" (Gal. 6:16; 3:7, 29; Rom. 2:29; 4:9; 9:6; Phil. 3:3.

Reconciliation in Bridal Imagery—Romans 7:1-6

"Do you not know, brothers—for I am speaking to men who know the law—that the law has authority over a man only as long as he is alive, but if her husband dies, she is released from the law of marriage. SO then, if she marries another man while her husband is still alive, she is called an adulteress, even though she marries another man. So, my brothers, you also died to the law through the body of Christ, that you might belong to another, to him who was raised from the dead, in order that we might bear fruit to Gods. For when we were controlled by the sinful nature, the sinful passions aroused by the law were at work in our bodies, wo that we bore fruit for death. But now, by dying to what once bound us, we have been released from the law so that we serve in the new way of the Spirit, and not in the old way of the written code."

This passage is another stepping stone to understand Paul's concept of the church's being wedded to Christ. By use of bridal imagery, Paul adds a new dimension to the meaning of reconciliation through Christ. Paul again uses marital imagery to illustrate that the church has passed out of the power of sin in order to become the bride of Christ. Paul writes both to the work of Christ and the responsibility of the church in regard to reconciliation.

In this passage, Paul begins by stating that when the husband dies, the woman is free to marry. This fact that death clears all scores was a universally known principle of law.

The main point of the illustration of the Law of the husband is that the death of the husband releases the woman from the bond of her husband. So a married woman is bound to her husband as long as he lives. When he dies, the bond is broken and she is released from the legal obligation and free to marry another.

Analogy of human marriage to divine reconciliation

In these verses, Paul begins the analogy with an example of human marriage and then proceeds to the divine marriage between Christ and the church. In order to follow the analogy more clearly, I want to point out four various aspects of this analogy:

1. The Wife= the true self which is permanent through all change

2. The First Husband =the sinful state before conversion to Christ

3. The "law of the Deceased Husband" = the law which allows the person to choose another spouse

4. The New Marriage= the union upon which the convert enters into a new relationship with Christ.

Wife as the church. - It is at verse four that Paul begins to apply the analogy of human marriage to the spiritual sphere of the church's relation to the Law and to Christ. The main focus of the analogy is the wife as she represents the church as a collective body and as individual church members. In this analogy, the wife is her one true self which remains permanent throughout all change but nevertheless passes through different experiences or phases. That is, she is pictured as a person who finds her existence both living under the law before conversion and being married to Christ after conversion. The wife in this analogy is the person who is in the process of owning both the "old person" and the "new person."

First husband. - The analogy of the first husband represents the old state before conversion to whom the wife was married at one time. In Paul's mind, the first husband was married to the law. This is what Paul means that the first husband was wedded to sin. Then he writes, "So my brothers, you also died to the law through the body of Christ that you might belong to another... But now, by dying to once bound us, we have been released from the law of sin so we may serve in the new way of the spirit.n Murray (1965) clarifies this idea when he states, "We are married to the law as the woman is to the husband and we cannot be released from the law until death occurs, just as the woman is not released until the husband dies.

Law of the husband. The law of the husband is the law which condemned the old state and it was that which held the wife captive to the first husband. Paul briefly introduced the analogy of slavery in verse six to show the function of law. Paul's picture of slavery was employed to reinforce the idea that the Christian is removed from his former sinful life and obedience to sin. The relationship between law and sin is mentioned repeatedly in Paul's writings. Paul does imply that the law is to be equated with sin. Nevertheless, the law prior to conversion, served to incite people to sin. Therefore, Paul writes that the law is closely associated with the fact of sin and disobedience.

New marriage. - The new marriage under this analog isrepresented as the union of the wife to Christ or reconciliation. However, the new marriage is not possible until there is death that frees the woman from the law of her former husband. Prior to understanding the new marriage, there is a death which Paul is referring to that makes the new marriage possible.

Death of the husband. - In Romans Six, Paul speaks of Christians having died with Christ (Romans 6:1-11). The effect of dying with Christ is that one is united with Christ. It is in this union with Christ that the Christian participates in a newness of life in which his members are no longer members of sin but instruments of God unto righteousness (Romans 6:13). Having said this, Paul attempts to make the meaning of dying even clearer by the analogy of marriage. In doing so, Paul speaks of the manner in which reconciliation 1S to take place between Christ and his bride, the church. Paul speaks to the promise of reconciliation that was declared by the Old Testament prophets where Yahweh promised to initiate a new marriage between himself and his adultress wife, Israel. She would once again become a pure virgin bride.

In regard to this matter of dying, believers in Christ are represented as dying with Christ and by that event, released from the bond of the law in order that we might be united to Hirn and raised with Hirn from death.

In staying within this analogy, there is a death which releases the bond just as decisively as the death of the Husband, and that death is our death to the Law in the death of Christ. This is the definitive dissolution corresponding to the death of the husband in the marital analogy.

The death that Paul is referring to is not the physical death of the whole self, but the death of the old self. The death of the old self was crucified with Christ and that death leaves a person free to marry a new wife. Believers take their place as it were with Christ upon the cross and their sinful nature was crucified with Christ. Believers share in the crucifixion of Christ and this releases them from their sinful past. Dodd (1932) recognizes the significance of Paul's teaching on dying when he writes,

> The Christian is dead in union with his crucified Lord. The crucified body of Christ made the Christian dead to the law—the body of Christ" means the actual body which was crucified. Paul took so seriously the idea of the

church as embodying the "corporate personality" of Christ that in the death of Christ on the cross he always saw the death of the whole people of God to sin, law and flesh... the result of this death, of Christ for us and of ourselves "in Hirn" is that we belong to Christ (as the wife belongs to her husband).

End of dying with Christ. - Freedom from the law by dying to the law is not an end in itself. Rather Paul writes that death to the law is directed to a positive end. The purpose designed in our being put to death to the law is to bear fruit for Christ. Paul writes, "that you should be joined to one another even to Him who was raised from the dead that you might bring forth fruit unto God." The purpose of the union with Christ is a relationship in which Believers might be fruitful to God in contrast to the former sinful passions. These sinful passions were working to bring forth fruit unto death which was prior to dying with Christ. Therefore, the idea of a fruitful marriage suggests that the result of conversion to Christ is a morally fruitful life.

Paul's use of the analogy of marriage in Romans 7:1-6 is of special importance. For it integrates Paul's thinking regarding reconciliation to Christ. This theme of reconciliation in the marital imagery has an intimate relation to the model for Christian marriage and marital reconciliation which Paul writes of in Ephesians 5:21-33. In using bridal imagery, Paul employs the divine model of marriage set forth in Ephesians. The divine model of marriage is the goal of reconciliation.

Authority, Love, and Unity in Bridal Imagery
--Ephesians 5:21-23

"Submit to one another out of reverence for Christ. Wives, submit to your husbands as to the Lord. For the husband is the head of the wife as Christ is the head of the church, his body, of which he is the Savior. Now as the church submits to Christ, so also wives should submit to their husbands in everything. Husbands, love your wives, just as Christ loved the church and gave himself up for her to make her holy, cleansing her by the washing with water through the word, and to present her to himself as a radiant church, without stain or winkle or any other blemish, but holy and blameless. In this same way, husbands ought to love their wives as their own bodies. He who loves his wife loves himself. After all, no one ever gated his own body, but he feeds and cares for it, just as Christ does the Church—for we are members of his body. For this reason a man will leave his father and mother and be united to his wife, and the two will become one flesh. This is a profound mystery—but I am talking about Christ and the church. However, each one of you also must love his wife as he loves himself, and the wife must respect her husband."

There is a context for this passage. In these verses, Paul's understanding of authority, love, and unity in the bridal imagery is crucial.

1. The model of authority

2. The model of love

3. The model of unity

Within these three models, there is a definite interplay and relatedness which concerns the husband and wife and with those parts which refer to Christ and the church.

Model of divine authority (Ephesians 5:21-24)

Paul begins his discourse on authority with the command for Christians to be subject to one another:

"Be subject to one another out of reverence to Christ [Ephesians 5:21]." The verb "submission" is the sense of voluntary yielding in love. The word "besubject" is not a suggestion, but an imperative command. Therefore, Paul's primary concern is that no one unjustly abuses another, but that all are ready to place the interest of others above one's own self. As it stands, it is a general admonition calling for the submission of each one to the other in the fear of Christ. In Philippians, Paul describes the idea of mutual subjection by saying, "Do nothing from selfishness or conceit but in humility count others better than yourselves. Let each of you look not only to his own interests, but also to the interest of others [Philippians 2:3-4]."

In Paul's plea for mutual subjection to one another, he does not destroy the principle of authority which is evident in the passages which follow regarding the relationships between husbands and wives, fathers and children, and masters and slaves. The principle of mutual subordination is not so applied as to destroy the complementary principle of authority. Paul knew from experience that the secret of maintaining joyful fellowship in the community was the order and discipline that come from the willing submission of one person to another. In attempting to apply this command to the human experience of marriage, there must be a willingness to serve one another, to learn from one another, and to be corrected by one another. This concept of authority applies to all human relationships regardless of age, class, race, or any other division. All authority finds its value in the understanding of the verb "subjection". Subjection is a verb that is always ordered under the authority of Christ. Therefore, the basis of this subjection is to be done out of respect for Christ, and not out of fear for Christ. The word reverence or "fear" of God is a common theme in Scripture. The "fear" of God, does not mean fright. Fear and reverence is understood best when we know that this love relationship was an initiative taken by God in Christ. Therefore, believers must always respond to this initiative in view of what God and Christ has done for us.

The call to submission in the fear of Christ is intended to be a loving response to an initial act of love taken upon by God in Christ. The best example of this concept of authority is when Jesus washed the disciples' feet. Jesus was given all authority on heaven and on earth and yet he stooped to the lowly position of a servant to wash the disciples' feet. We know that Jesus and the father and the Holy Spirit are all equal and yet, on many occasions, Jesus said "not my will, but thy will be done" when praying to Father God. After washing the disciples' feet, Jesus said, "Go and do likewise". Following the general exhortation and instruction to mutual concern, Paul sets forth instructions for the Christian household. He begins with an address to the wives.

> Wives be subject to your husbands, as to the Lord. For the husband is the head of the wife as Christ is the head of the Church, His body, and is Himself its Savior. As the Church is subject to Christ so let wives also be subject in everything to their husbands [Ephesians 5:22-24].

In the original Greek text, the verb instructing wives to be subject to their husbands is not included in verse twenty-two! Therefore, subjection is obviously intended to carryover from its participial use in the previous verse. In any case, thus, it is clearly understood that the wives are called to be devoted to their husbands exactly in the same way that Christians are commanded to selflessness and service. In addressing the wives, Paul here intends that the command to be subject to their husbands has the same meaning as the command in the preceding verse, i.e., voluntary yielding in love in response to the loving initiative on behalf of the husband.

I now want to say more about the word "submissive". First of all, it is a command to be submissive. Paul's command for wives "to be subject" to their husbands is a sensitive topic. To address this subject, it is imperative to understand what Paul interprets "subjection" to mean in the context of the analogy of Christ as head of the church. Paul instructs husbands and wives to see their relationship as following the pattern of the relationship between Christ and His church. Authority is a good word. It is a concept that is old as God. It is a concept that is necessary for love, unity, and equality. Paul sees in the marriage relationship then a type of unity in a common life which is God's ultimate purpose in creation and which is realized in its absolute form in the union of Christ with the Church The relation of husband and wife, like that of Christ to the Church, points to unity included in the idea of creation.

The analogy of the union of Christ and His church calls for an equality between them even in the face of the hierarchical command to headship and authority which affects the marital union as well. In this Union the church appears as a person equal in position with Christ where the church stands on the same level as Christ. Thus, the church is on the one hand, an independent person, the Object of Christ's love, and on the other hand, so closely connected with Him, the Head, the Savior, that together they constitute a unity. Paul emphasized the equality between husband and wife: "There is neither male nor female, for you are all one in Christ Jesus [Galatians 3:28]." Paul also pleads for a true mutuality in the physical sexual relation (I Corinthians 7:3-5). I will speak more of this in a later chapter.

Furthermore, the freedom of mutual consent and covenant-making found both in the marital union and in the union of Christ and His church speaks of a mutual respect and equality one has toward another. Under the gospel of Christ mutual submission is inseparable from true love. A person is one created in the image of God with powers to say "yes" and "no". A love union involves an "I will" on both sides. A free "yes" is never produced by tyrannical power. It only comes by wooing and by grace.

Nevertheless, in the family and in the church, there must be leadership to maintain its order and its unity. The responsibility of leadership belongs to the husband and to Christ and their authority must be accepted. Likewise, there is a responsibility on the behalf of the wife and the church to accept the authority of the husband and of Christ. Paul is reminding husbands and wives of their duties, not their rights.

In the case of the wives, the duty is that of submitting themselves to their husbands. When it is said that Christ is the head of the church, two things are implied; the responsibility he accepts for the church and the church's responsibility toward him. There are comparable implications in the marriage relationship.

The command to the wife to be subject to her husband does not mean that the husband has the authority to command what he pleases. Rather, the wife is to be submissive to one whose duty to her is nothing less than self-giving love. The message of this passage is that women should devote themselves to their husbands so that the unity of the marriage may be most fully realized. The real message of the wife's "giving herself" completely to the husband. Again, wives devote themselves to a loving husband, and what the husband has done for them. Paul saw the need for the principle of order in both marriage and the church without diminishing in any way the intrinsic worth and dignity of the wife or the church.

Christ the husband as Savior.—Not only are both husband and Christ assigned headship, they also must assume their task as Savior. Now please note the difference between Christ and the husband. The difference, is that Christ is Himself the Savior. A man is the head of the wife, even as Christ is the head of the church, although there is a vast difference. Since Christ is Himself the Savior of the church. Christ is the head of the church. The husband does not hold towards the wife the unapproachable preeminence which Christ holds toward the church as the Savior! Saint Paul places the relationship of Christ to His church on a much higher level than that of the husband to his wife.

The difference between Christ and the husband is that God who is the author of salvation through Christ Jesus. Nevertheless, the fact that Paul uses this analogy does not necessarily mean the difference is so far removed from the role of the husband in being the "savior" of his wife. The husband is the savior of the wife in the sense that he is the provider and the preserver of his wife. Jesus Christs' authority over the church is used to protect and preserve the church from the disintegrating effects of sin and the assaults of Satanic abuse. In a certain sense, the husband has a sacrificial concern for his wife. The parallel, however, on a much lower level, the husband's loving and sacrificial concern for the welfare of his wife is like that of Christ's love for his church. In a similar way, the husband is the protector of his wife.

Model of divine love—Ephesians 5:25-27

Having addressed the wives, Paul now directs his attention to husbands. The command of God for husbands is to love their wives as Christ loved the church. "Husbands, love your wives, even as Christ loved the church [Ephesians 5:25]." The quality of love husbands are to give their wives is a self-sacrificing love.

The husband's love for his wife has as its model a love like Christ for his church—a love capable of suffering and dying for the wife. The husband's love toward his bride is measured by a superlative standard of self-sacrifice when it is likened to that of Christ for his church. Paul wants husbands to love their wives with a love that is totally unselfish. A love that seeks not his own satisfaction but strives for the highest good of his wife.

Self-Sacrificing Love

The husband's love for his wife is a love that is much more than affection or mere attraction. Rather, it is a love which involves his active and self-sacrificing concern for her wellbeing. The husband's love is modeled after the love of Christ which is a self-giving love. Christ gave himself up for the church and the inference is that there is no sacrifice which a husband should not be prepared to make, even the sacrifice of his own life for his wife.

Purpose of Self-Giving Love

The love Christ has for the church was not only sacrificial but it was also a love which led to sanctification, The death of Christ was not an end in itself, rather it was directed to an end for the church. The purpose of Christ's death is given in Ephesians 5:26:

"That he might sanctify her, having cleansed her by the washing of water with the word, that he might present the church to Himself in splendor, without spot or wrinkle or any such thing. That she might be holy and without blemish.

In regard to the above text there are three purpose clauses:

1. To sanctify the church

2. To present the church to himself

3. That it may continue to be holy, and without blemish

These three purposes are correlative with the already developed bridal imagery. In Jewish marriage customs, the bride is also prepared and presented to her husband and then continues to be in fellowship with him. The death of Christ has a cleansing function in connection with sanctification. The fact that sanctification is a cleansing process implies the idea of a changed relationship to God on behalf of the church, his bride. By sanctification, the church is separated from what is profane and set in a consecrated state. As Christ dies and resurrects, there is a clear idea of "setting apart". The idea is the deliverance from sin and guilt through the cleansing blood of Christ and baptism.

It appears that Paul's reference to baptism in the context of bridal imagery underscores the thought that cleansing is brought about only through the work of Christ. This thought stands in striking contrast to the bridal bath. The bridal bath was customarily considered a work of self-cleansing accomplished by the bride herself. In bridal customs, it was the bride who prepared herself for her husband. Her cleansing activity was found in and of herself. Now, there is a striking difference between the bath of the bride and the bath effected by Christ in baptism.

In Jewish wedding customs, A bride makes preparation for her marriage that she may appear before her husband in all her beauty so the church is to appear before her heavenly bridegroom. In the case of the Church, the bride can do nothing of herself to make herself beautiful in the eyes of God. The Church can do nothing of herself to make herself beautiful in the eyes of God. Of necessity it is all the work of the Lord Jesus Christ. The Church can only be without spot or wrinkle by the sanctifying and renewing work of Christ.

The second purpose clause is to present the church to himself. Not only does the death of Christ sanctify the church but the church is also to be presented to God. This is another reason that Christ gave himself up for the church. The meaning here is to place her beside himself. To be near him. To set her at hand. Christ is at once the bridegroom who receives the bride and presents her to himself.

There is an important context to be understood here. In the analogy, the bride is both equal and there is a command to be submissive. The equality is understood as Christ places the Church alongside himself. The Church is equal and in a position of honor. As believers, we all know and confess the equality of the Father Son and Holy Spirit, the Holy Trinity. This equality has never been shattered, even when Christ was on earth. It is true that Christ became human. It is also true that in his equality with the Father, he repeatedly said, "Not my will but thy will be done". In the nature of this supreme equality, there is also a divine submission to the Father's will. Therefore, there is no interruption or corruption in the equality and honor in which the trinity is based.

In Jewish customs, the honor and purity of the bride is analogous to Christ and his church, the bride. Therefore, when the church is presented to Christ, it has the underlying theme of reconciliation. Paul writes in Colossians 1:21-22:

> And you who were once estranged and hostile in mind, doing evil deeds, he has now reconciled you in his body of flesh by his death in order to present you holy and blameless and irreproachable before him.

In truth, this is a reference to reconciliation resulting from Christ's sacrifice. For those of you who are in an estranged or troubled marriage, this should provide hope and encouragement to whatever your situation may be.

In regard to the third clause, the Church is to be holy and without blemish which is the process of sanctification. In this clause, Paul stresses the quality of life in which the church must continue to live as a response to her reconciliation. In conclusion, the Church strives to live a life style which looks back to the saving event of Jesus Christ on the cross and at the same time looks forward to an ethical life of faithfulness.

You all know that the Last Supper was a Passover supper. When Jesus broke the bread and poured out the wine, he said, "This is a new covenantu. If this is a new covenant, what is the old covenant? The old covenant was the giving and receiving of the Ten Commandments. The new covenant was open to all people of any race, tribe, nation, or people.

And, the new covenant was very simple. You all know what it is. Love the Lord your God, with all your heart, mind, soul, and strength, and love your neighbor as yourself. If we follow the law of the new covenant, it will lead to a life of sanctification and renewal.

Model of divine unity (Ephesians 5:28-33)

The model for unity in the marital relation is expressed in the final verse of this passage:

> "In this same way, husbands ought to love their wives as their own bodies. He who loves his wife loves himself. After all, no one ever hated his own body, but he feeds and cares for it, just as Christ does the church—for we are members of his body. For this reason a man will leave his father and mother and be united to his wife, and the two will become one flesh. This is a profound mystery—but I

am talking about Christ and the church. However, each one of you also must love his wife as he loves himself, and the wife must respect her husband."

These verses are very significant in developing the theme of unity in marriage. Paul writes, ''Even so husbands should love their wives as their own bodies [Ephesians 5:28]''. Even in the very first book of the Bible, Genesis, God writes, "The two shall become one flesh".

Paul write that this is a great mystery. When a man and his wife become one flesh, Paul can speak of the wives being the same as the bodies of the husbands. This means that a man's wife is the same as his own body. Paul continues to write that no man ever hates his own flesh, but nourishes it and cherishes it. Husbands and wives together share a unity which is expressed in terms of self-care for the body. Paul understands that a man and his wife become one flesh. He regards the love to one's wife as an extension of his own self-love. Just as a man would nourish and cherish his own body, he needs to care for his wife with equal concern.

Having stated this, Paul continues to explain that it is a general law of nature for most men to nourish and cherish their own flesh for the purpose of gaining maturity. It seems only natural for a person to be careful on how they care for themselves. Hopefully, both men and women will continue to be nourishing themselves from one stage to another as they mature in the three score and ten years that are allotted to them on this earth.

In addition, Paul uses another word. That word is "cherish". This word primarily means to foster the body with tender care and keep it warm. It also means to cover and protect the body.

A husband's love leads him to regard her welfare as his own and to feel that all that concerns her as if it concerned himself. Paul's real thought is that the union in marriage is like that of Christ and the church. Christ is related to the church as the head is to the body, and the relation of man and wife ought to be just as close.

Paul again draws attention to an analogy of this love with the union Christ has with this church. Just as Christ nourishes and cherishes the church, believers are assured of Christ's compassionate care. The metaphor used to describe this union is that of an organic living body. Just as the church is a veritable part of the body of Christ, there is also the idea of the close unity between husbands and wives. There is a divine purpose in human marriage. The wife becomes a part of the very life of her husband and he nourishes and cherishes her, even so the Lord does to us as members of himself, we are part of his own life. The thought which Paul is leading up to finds its capstone in verse thirty-one: "For this reason a man shall leave his father and mother and be joined to his wife and the two shall become one." This verse is a quotation from Genesis 2:24. The verse in Genesis appears to be influencing the entire thought of Paul's writing in regard to the idea of unity within marriage.

A careful study of this unity begins with the idea of a man leaving his father and mother. A husband will leave his mother and father at some point in the future and cleave to his wife. Cleaving here means that the husband will adhere closely to his wife, be faithfully devoted to his wife, and join his wife in all future endeavors. Marriage, then, indicates a new bond between husbands and wives. Prior to marriage, the closest bond a man and woman has is that to their parents. Marriage is a new bond and the most intimate relation now is between husband and wife. It is the husband's love for his wife as his own body which draws the two individuals into a one flesh relation. This mysterious union is realized in the act of giving, both on a human level and the divine Christ-church relation. In both the marital and the Christ-church relation, the mysterious unity of husband and wife is realized through their participation in an act of the body which enables them to share each other's vital forces.

Paul regarded the union of two into one flesh as a great mystery. This is not to be understood as a mystery implying something hidden and unknown, but rather a mystery which is of profound importance. This mystery is a revelation of spiritual truth made to those who are prepared to receive it. Here the mystery is the revelation of the nature of human marriage, the union of two persons into one flesh. This perfect unity is realized fully in the union of Jesus Christ and the church.

Summary

Paul's use of bridal imagery describes the basis and the aim of reconciliation. The basis for reconciliation in the Christ-church relationship is centered in the redeeming work of Christ's death on the cross. The aim of reconciliation in the Christ-church relationship is (a) the recognition and proper exercise of authority, (b) the awareness and the acceptance of the self-giving love of Christ in the everyday life of the church, and (c) the sharing of one another's vital forces which establishes a divine unity. Marriages patterned after the Christ-church relationship involve a proper understanding of authority, the presence of self-giving love, and the maintaining of unity between husband and wife.

CHAPTER IV

PRINCIPLES OF INTEGRITY THERAPY

In my attempt to integrate the principles for reconciliation, I want to correlate the general concepts of Integrity Therapy with our understanding of the Biblical teaching for marital reconciliation. Integrity Therapy was originated by 0. Hobart Mowrer. For this purpose, I have selected selections from the book written by J.W. Drakeford (1967) entitled Integrity Therapy. This book was selected because it best describes the concepts of Integrity Therapy.

Hobart Mowrer had the very productive and curious career of any psychologist in the 20 Century. He himself struggled with severe mental illness and anxiety. In the 1940's he became interested with the teachings of Christianity. He claimed that anxiety was caused by repressed guilt that came from wrong behavior and claimed that sin was responsible for nearly all psychological problems. H also claimed that ethical and moral living combined with confession of wrongdoing could prevent mental illness. In addition, this could also bring about reconciliation in broken relationships. He is the perfect psychologist to integrate biblical principles of marital reconciliation with sound psychological principle.

Hobart Mowrer had a very high respect for Drakeford's book, Integrity Therapy. Mowrer writes, "there is now a sizable and growing literature on Integrity Groups-but probably the best integrated, synoptic description is to be found in Drakeford's book, Integrity Therapy. In this regard, Drakeford writes,

> "Mowrer's formulations are at least parallel with many Biblical statements made long before the so called 'secular concepts' were enunciated it must be obvious to the open-minded reader that integrity therapy follows not only the letter but also the spirit of the Bible". [P.143]

Human Failure and Responsibility

To isolate and describe the various concepts of Integrity Therapy, it must be understood that the component parts of this system are internally related to each other. Dr. Mowrer describes this as a process in which one aspect affects another aspect. Together this process forms a series of events which may be described as a chain reaction sequence. Human failure or wrongdoing gives rise to conscience, conscience gives rise to guilt, guilt gives rise to anxiety. Dr. Mowrer has advanced the formulation that a person who has acted in contradiction to his internalized standards experiences a violation of conscience which gives rise to guilt. Drakeford writes, "Each person has a conscience, or value system, the violation of which gives rise to guilt. This condition is not a sickness but a result of his wrongdoing and irresponsibility". In connection with personal wrongdoing, Integrity Therapy believes in the acceptance of personal responsibility for behavior. By assuming personal responsibility, Integrity Therapy believes that every individual has the free choice of making personal decisions. In relation with this, Drakeford writes,

> "Integrity Therapy rejects all deterministic theories which make man a victim of heredity, environment or any other force. Every individual is answerable for himself and exercises his responsibility in making his personal decision [P.9]

Conscience and Guilt

Conscience plays an important role in the theory of Integrity Therapy. Conscience may best be described as functioning for each person as a custom-made measuring gauge of conduct and values. Drakeford (1967) writes,

> Distinctly a human phenomenon, man_looks over his life and behavior patterns, evaluating and passing judgment on them. His behavior is either in conformity with, or in conflict with, his value system. Conscience is the sensitive, flickering needle which measures the relationship of conduct and values. [P.15]

Integrity Therapy recognizes that conscience comes is 'assorted sizes'. Values which are placed on behavior vary from one individual to another. It is recognized that there are individuals whose conscience is inoperable, and values placed on conduct are nonexistent. This would include sociopaths and some selected narcissists.

Because Integrity Therapy places such importance on the function of conscience, it readily recognizes the problem of the sociopath. Drakeford acknowledges this when he writes, 11Practitioners of Integrity Therapy have been ready to acknowledge the problem of the sociopath. Consequently, the use of an Integrity Therapy technique does not have a very hopeful prognosis". [P.65]

As Drakeford aptly writes, conscience serves both a negative and positive function. Not only does conscience inform a person of behavior which should not be followed, but it also informs a person of behavior which should be followed. When conscience fails in its function to prevent actions contrary to a person's values, the resulting consequence will be guilt. The interplay of conscience and guilt is important to carefully distinguish between 'real guilt'and 'guilty feelings'.

"Sometimes conscience expresses itself in 'affective language'. Persons may experience 'guilt feelings'. Integrity

Therapy practitioners are quick to point out that it is not 'guilt feelings' but guilt, pure and simple, which is causing the trouble. Depression and gloom are one of the many ways guilt is communicated. Nevertheless, depression is probably the most frequently encountered indication of an affected conscience".

In reference to the presence of guilt in the process of Integrity Therapy, guilt has its negative function insofar as guilt may cause various levels of anguish. Guilt is often unrelenting and a tyrannical force, creating misery and unhappiness for a person. When guilt which has not been •paid for', it is a source of a person's anxiety.

"Unfaced guilt is then the great black mailer. The victims hide their failures by putting on a brave face to the world. But people are pressured in myriad ways to make payments to guarantee that their secret will not be revealed".

I believe that hiding is a curse. In the Garden of Eden, Adam and Eve tried to hide. Their hiding was motivated by guilt and shame. They tried to pretend but it didn't work. In their attempt to hide, they only found a place of fear and anxiety. And then the dreadful words that God said to Adam, "Adam, where are you?" God knew exactly where Adam was geographically, but he wanted to know what was happening in his soul. Therefore, it must be recognized that unfaced guilt is a highly negative force in a person's life.

Integrity Therapy also believes in the constructive use of guilt. Real acknowledgement of guilt has a very positive outcome.

In the early church, Saint Paul said that true community is when people love each other genuinely. Paul writes that this early community met together with glad and sincere hearts. I suspect that they learned how to stop pretending and be authentic versions of themselves. True love for one another has always been God's plan for human life and marriage.

Imagine what your marriage would be like if all pretense was gone and imagine the freedom if there was complete openness and honesty. This is God's plan for marriage. As stated, before in this book, guilt has an intimate relationship with the great doctrines of the Christian faith. The Christian faith promises atonement, reconciliation, justification, and forgiveness of sin. Guilt is the raw subject material out of which spiritual freedom is forged. Dealing with and accounting for confessed guilt produces freedom. It helps marital partners to realize how valuable they are and how they have been cheating themsel es and their partner. Fortunately, people who tire of extortion and finally come clean with their shameful stories, often discover new courage in continuing to admit the transgressions that they have committed. They find themselves in an unexpected climate of worthwhile living. Guilt ,can be the wonderful instrument for making a person into a new and meaningful partner. It is a great blessing to not live in shame and anxiety.

Concealment versus Confession

In facing the problem of guilt, perhaps the most common route followed is the practice of deception and concealment. Adam and Eve tried to hide from God. Such attempts to conceal guilt spring from the wish to avoid the work, self-sacrifice, and discipline involved in keeping a contract with the values placed on behavior. Integrity Therapy believes that a person who has acted in contradiction to his internalized standards, will often try to avoid the consequences of his act by concealing his guilt. Integrity Therapy believes that concealed guilt is the cause for various levels of anxiety. In this secrecy, gui t throws up symptoms of varying degrees of severity, from vague discomfort to complete immobilization.

As an antidote to concealed guilt, Integrity Therapy views openness and honesty with 'significant others' as a step toward healing. As secrecy brought on a person's trouble and separated them from other people, so openness with 'significant others' is the individual's first step on the road back to reconciliation. Openness and honesty expressing itself in the form of confession.

Dr. Mowrer states,

> "When a person has violated a contract and then tries to avoid the consequences by concealment, confession is the first step which, if the outcome is to be maximally constructive, mut be followed by restitution".

Confession has both a negative and positive value attached to it. From a negative perspective, confession may be only an emotional release of feeling. This may not be of any value in itself. For some people, cheap confession may be a fleeting feeling of catharsis. Integrity Therapy attempts to go beyond these negative experiences.

From a positive perspective, open and honest confession recognizes the genuine feelings of embarrassment released by personal admission of wrong behavior. In addition, Integrity Therapy believes that confession should also motivate.a person to do something about their situation. A truly effective confession is reflected in a changed lifestyle. This is the positive side. Confession is not only made with the mouth, but also completed by a change in behavior.

Now there is also a problem with confession. Confession has often been and can be misused by persons who wish to harm others or even themselves. Confession which does not take into consideration such factors as timing, persons confessed to, and place of confession can be dangerous and cause more problems than it originally hoped to solve. Therefore, the place of confession calls for certain considerations for it to be effective.

> "Confession is not complaining. Complaining generally focuses on the emotions. The subject spends the time describing how he feels, and it is in reality, a bath of self-pity. Integrity Therapy does not see any therapeutic value in complai i g, and it is not valid.
>
> Secondly, Confession is not blaming other people for problems and difficulties-it is possible, by the process of rationalization to build up a very plausible argument

blaming other people for their failures. This is not a confession.

Thirdly, Confession focuses on weaknesses rather than strengths. To admit one's failure is probably the indication of a humility necessary for any real honesty and willingness to learn from our bad behavior. For a real confessional experience to be of value, it must focus on the person's shortcomings and failures.

Fourthly, sometimes confessions can be made for other people! Many people are willing to confess by telling another person's story. If confession is to be effective, it must be about oneself and not others.

Confession is made to 'significant others'. The real crux of the matter is to know to whom to confess. It would be ridiculous to tell every person one meets about transgressions. Integrity Therapy never advocates indiscriminate confession". [P.97]

And lastly, Confession is willingness to come under the judgment of our fellows. Some people are inhibited by the fear that if they become open and acknowledge their failures, the person to whom they confess will not understand, or will look down on them in contempt. We often overlook the potency of a gesture of honesty in which weaknesses are acknowledged. When we open our lives to the judgment of others, we are often amazed at their reactions. Within this matrix, we discover ourselves and the strength of the interest of our fellows. Choose carefully who you confess to. Just as covering up, concealing, and disguising bring distress; the way back through openness and self-disclosure bring healing and a sense of well-being".

Restitution

The significance of restitution in Integrity Therapy is of great importance. As has already been stated, Integrity Therapy believes confession to be of great significance; by itself, and it is not sufficient. For personal confession to be of any value, it must be followed with the desire to amend previous lifestyles. Restitution finds expression in a person's willingness to amend their lives in their actual behavior.

Confession and Restitution is only one stage in an ongoing process which includes a plan of action to achieve its therapeutic objective.

So, in conclusion, there is no magic in admitting 'who we are' to one person unless we progressively extend our openness to significant others in our lives and take steps to change our behavior and rectify past injustices.

Furthermore, in the process of Integrity Therapy, the main emphasis is on the volitional level of life. Confession, restitution and putting things back, must be motivated by a personal choice. That is, people must do something, work at it, if they are to satisfy the demands of their conscience. Restitution may express itself in various ways according to the demand of each individual's conscience.

Each individual must discover for themselves just what is their own personal penance and undertake a program of action for restitution. Restitution is not intended to show others a life of change; rather, restitution has as its goal true forgiveness. This often results in a fundamental change of character.

Dr. Drakeford states,

"There is a sense in which all sin is against God and only He can forgive the sins of men and women. But it is one thing for God to forgive and another for the sinner to know that he is forgiven. It frequently requires some plan for 'putting things back' before we can experience real forgiveness. Most people need to see visible evidence or participate in an act which gives them an inward sense that they really are made whole again".

In my attempt to make this concept clear, I want to share a brief story of one of my clients. My client was struggling greatly with his need to make things right with the person that he had offended. He wrote out his confession, he wrote out what he was going to say to the offended party. He practiced reading his confession in front of his mirror. After all this hard work, he finally called the offended party and made his verbal and sincere apology. He wasn't exactly sure what to expect. And to his disappointment, the wounded friend simply blew him off. The person that he apologized to said, "Oh, that's no problem"! My client then experienced a new wound. He was devalued and diminished by the response of the offended party.

Confession and making things right with others are not easy. Like my client, it takes a lot of hard work. I would like to think that when we make confession to God, God reacts with great delight and good will. I believe that God would congratulate the sinner and acknowledge the work and the effort he put into making his confession.

Involvement with Others

The statement, "you alone can do it, but you can't do it alone" capsulates the philosophy behind Integrity Therapy. Reconciliation in terms of Integrity Therapy involves both an individual responsibility and collective responsibility. One of the Twelve Steps in AA is, "Having written a fearless and courageous moral inventory of one's life, you are asked to share this inventory with another human being". Telling another human person, the most vulnerable aspects of our lives leads us to the deepest disclosure of true intimacy. At this point, we are ready to unveil the areas of failure or embarrassment that are most intimate and secret. This type of disclosure should not be entered into lightly. Jesus .told us that we should love all people. Nevertheless, we should only choose a proven friend to entrust the secrets of the heart. To understand this deliberate self-disclosure, Jesus said, "I no longer call you servants, for a servant does not know what the Master is doing. But I have called you 'friends', for everything I heard from my Father, I have made known to you". Jesus modeled this deep disclosure to only a few trusted friends.

People are not likely to change with the concern and help of others. Change involves a great deal of anguish to share and trust in some type of community or group. The process of socialization with others in Integrity Therapy can best be realized within a small group. Integrity Therapy feels that the group setting provides the matr.ix within which one can learn the balance between dependence and independence. The group has various advantages for people who want healing, such as:

-The group provides a situation in many ways similar to the social milieu in which the problems developed [P.109]. This may include family, work or school.

-Small groups provide, "troubled people with an opportunity to learn skills in helping other people.

-Participation in small groups affords people to learn attitudes of trustfulness and faith.

-Small group experiences break down the sense of isolation and aloneness.

-And sometimes, individuals will learn to look at their problem from an entirely different perspective.

-The small group process often produces people with unusual gifts of group leadership previously undiscovered.

Integrity Therapy views involvement with others as one of its major concepts. It views the road to healing and restoration as a life-long process, a process which continues to build a person even after his period of crisis may be over. Consequently, a person's involvement with other people becomes in a sense a 'mission' whereby the process of becoming an authentic person is accomplished by sharing the Reconciliation Process with others. One receives by giving. "The only way to continue as a truly authentic person is not only to remain open and make restitution, but also to feel a responsibility to carry the message of Hope and Reconciliation to other broken people.

In conclusion, Integrity Therapy provides. a setting in which healing is possible through acknowledging guilt and assuming responsible action for restitution. The major principle which pervades the scope of this system is the emphasis on personal openness and honesty, responsibility and involvement.

Biblical Principles for Reconciliation

This book is an attempt to present biblical principles for reconciliation. Reconciliation between God and his covenant people is the main theme of the entire word of God. As stated before, this work of reconciliation was completed by the death and resurrection of the Lord Jesus Christ. These are also biblical principles for marital reconciliation. The analogy between human marriage and the marital theme in the bible makes sense. Reconciliation between God and his people is the theme of the entire word of God.

Reconciliation between a broken marriage is always God's purpose for the unhappy couple. Unfortunately, all broken marriages don't always experience reconciliation. This is a painful truth. Therefore, there are many pitfalls when we compare God's marriage to his people with broken marriages, between husbands and wives.

There are many parallels between divine marriage and human marriage. Nevertheless, not all parallels are accurate. In the first place, it would be wrong to conclude that the wife is responsible for the broken marital-relationship. And it would be wrong to blame the husband for the cause of the breakdown in marriage. Marriages in need of reconciliation are not necessarily caused by one partner. Both partners are capable and culpable of bringing about discord in marriage. The principles which follow are those which we find in the Bible.

Marriage is by Free Choice

This study mentions the significance of partners choosing one another as a basis for marriage. In the Old Testament, there is a picture of God choosing Israel and asking her to become partners with Him (see Exodus 19:3-5). In response to God's covenantal invitation, Israel, in turn, freely chooses to enter into covenant with God (Exodus 19:10-17).

Marriage partners must by their own free volition, choose to marry one another. In the act of freely choosing one another, they are at the same time acknowledging and agreeing to the written, spoken, and assumed responsibilities incurred by each for the establishment of marriage. Barth (1968) writes,

"A further standpoint, more painful but quite indispensable, for the establishment of a love which can support marriage is offered by the fact that for the marriage and for the love of two persons the agreement of both is requi red... love cannot be forced. It is a gift which comes to two persons, and as such it exercises its compulsion on both sides or else it is not love and is useless for the founding of marriage" [p.52].

Free choice is the bedrock of g1v1ng and receiving sacred vows in marriage. Regarding this concept of freely choosing one another, free choice establishes a sacred covenant between people entering marriage. Both marital partners are therefore responsible for keeping the terms of their sacred vows. Regarding the concept of free choice, 0. Hobart Mowr r writes,

"Virtually every human interaction is on the basis of contracts, understood agreements, formal or informal, the structure of our personalities, indeed our very identities are contractua l ly determined... When we thus see how indispensable and ubiquitous contracted agreements are in normal human existence, it follows almost axiomatically that persons who refuse to make contracts or who make them and then secretly or openly violate them will experience life very differently from the way in which responsible authentic cooperative persons do". [pp.15-16]

In a similar way, Jesus stands at the door and knocks. Jesus never forces his way into the human heart. It is only by our free will that we open the door and enter intc:, a loving relationship with him. When we enter a relationship with Jesus, by our free choice, we instantly become the Bride of Christ.

The Call to Remember

There is a sweetness in recalling the early days of our first love. In this same manner, the prophets of the Old Testament called Israel to remember the time when she was 'married' to the Lord. It was hoped that in the act of remembering, she would bring back into her consciousness the days when her relationship with God was pleasant. By recalling Israel's early days with the Lord, the prophets were able to provide a, striking contrast between the pleasant days of love and the present anguish of alienation. Revisiting her first 'love' would hopefully encourage Israel to re-establish her loyalty to her husband.

Likewise, it is often necessary in the process of ma ital reconciliation for the couple to recall the days of their early love. The memory of such love may suggest the investment that each has in the relationship. Once this is realized, the couple may be more reluctant to dissolve their relationship. The memory of early love may also encourage the couple to re-capture once again the love they once had.

In dealing with the past, Integrity Therapy might not support such activities of reflection. The focus of Integrity Therapy centers on a person's present behavior and activity. The history of a person's life is de-emphasized. Reality Therapy as set forth by William Glasser seems to be commensurate with Integrity Therapy. In both therapies, the primary attention is centered on present behavior.

Alienation in Marriage

The prophet Hosea spoke clearly regarding the contention God had with Israel. The cause of the broken relationship was the failure of Israel to observe the terms of the covenantal contract1which she voluntarily agrees to obey. Hosea writes, "There is no faithfulness of kindness: and no knowledge of God in the land: there is swearing, lying, killing, stealing and committing adultery". [Hosea 4:1-2] Together, all these activities represent a complete disregard for the terms of the relationship between Israel and God. The result of such blatant disregard for a once agreed upon covenant brought alienation and estrangement into the relationship.

As has already been mentioned, every relationship.has its mutual terms of which people agree upon. This is also true for marriage partners. It might appear that marriage partners have more intense and numerous vows and contract agreements than most human relationships (i.e., fidelity, support, finances, communication, control and many more). Alienation and estrangement also occur within marriage when the marital contracts are not observed or kept by either partner.

Confession and Reconciliation

Reconciliation between two parties can be defined as a new stage of personal relationship in which previous hostility of mind or estrangement has been put away in some decisive act. This decisive act is confession. In Old Testament marital imagery, this 'decisive act' was for Israel to acknowledge her guilt and to return again to the Lord. (Hosea 5:15-6:1). For this therapeutic process to occur, there must be a willingness on behalf of Israel to confess her sins with a genuine penitent heart. Since it was Israel who willingly broke the covenant, it was also Israel's responsibility to openly confess to God her failure to keep the terms of the covenant.

Even though it is recognized that Israel has a responsibility to confess her sins, God nonetheless plays an active role in the process of reconciliation. In the first place, it is God who actively provides a means of reconciliation and .takes the initiative for reconciliation to occur. The initiative taken by God was expressed in various ways. God took the initiative by sending His prophets to warn and counsel Israel. God took the initiative by confronting Israel with her failure to keep the covenant obligations. He placed before Israel, the evidence of her guilt. At long last, God took the initiative in openly expressing His anger and judgment upon Israel. It is interesting to note here that anger is also an avenue towards healing and reconciliation between two estranged persons. Anger is the positive side of reconciliation. Finally, her persistent rebellion, God continued His quest for her love in the form of a punishment. The punishment was her return into exile and God separating Himself from her for a season. Israel may have rejected God, but God has not rejected Israel.

In reference to marital reconciliation, genuine confession of failure to keep agreed contracts is the one decisive act which proves to be the most healing and cleansing experience. However, confession on behalf of the offending party does not utomatically. Not only. does the offending party have a responsibility to confess the offense, but it is also the responsibility of the offended partner to involve himself actively in bringing about the one decisive act which will restore the broken marriage. In the marital analogy, God provides a pattern which the offended partner may follow. Such activities w uld include patience and longsuffering, an openness to willingly point out grievances, and engagement in confrontation. If after all attempts, however, to attain reconciliation fail, there may be an open expression of anger as the result of personal hurt.

In the integrity group therapy model, many of these same concepts are present. Integrity groups provide a setting where members may 'reach out' to other members. Reaching out provides the opportunity for one to take the initiative in the process of healing. It provides the opportunity for open confrontation. It provides members with the free expression of anger over personal hurts.

Such activities taken on by the group are all done in the hope of bringing a person to admit openly and honestly his weaknesses and failures. Integrity Therapy views confession of guilt to be the avenue for healthy relationship and personal growth. In speaking of integrity groups, Mowrer (1972) writes, "There may be a good deal of confrontation and encountering-but there is always a lot of support, if and when it is indicated" [p.18].

As has already been noted, openness and honesty, especially in the area of confession of one's weaknesses and failures to various contractual agreements, are the main features of Integrity Therapy. Openness with significant others is the individual's first step on the road back to reconciliation. In the case of marital partners seeking reconciliation, open confession of one another's failures to the marriage may lead to the rebirth of love and provide restoration. However, this study recognizes Mowrer's principle of confession 'to the significant others' does not adequately describe the full measure of reconciliation. Integrity Therapy omits the forgiveness and restoration which was accomplished through the atonement with the death and resurrection of Christ. Mowrer's theories are very helpful, but I like to think of them as an 'unfinished symphony' because they leave out the forgiveness which comes from God through Christ. There is also the need for the deliverance from guilt in terms of God's perspective.

In our current culture, confession is tricky. Confession of guilt is not high on the list in our present-day society. When our unhappy couple violates their vows to one another, it creates big problems and prevents them from the reconciliation that they need through the confession of wrongdoing. Unfortunately, our culture does not support acknowledging guilt. It's easy for our culture to broaden its morality to include wrongdoing as acceptabl.e behavior. Our culture today uses both subtle and not-so-subtle powers. Our culture promotes wrongdoing to be viewed as friendly and alluring behavior. Our culture is seductive. Seduction has the quality of being powerfully and mysteriously attractive which leads us away from experiencing true guilt. When we are barred from experiencing true guilt, we will find sin to be attractive and fascinating. This unfortunately has the power to charm people into sin and bring them into spiritual disaster.

This can distract Christians from being faithful and loyal to their spouses. In addition, allowing this deception of accepting the sin as 'normal behavior' may have far reaching consequences as it may turn people away from their wholehearted devotion to the Lord Jesus Christ.

Restitution and Reconciliation

Very closely related to the biblical concept of confession is the concept of restitution for wrong behavior. Restitution is defined as that activity which follows a genuine confession. Restitution is a resolve by the offending party to 'put things back'. As it has already been shown that sanctification is the goal, a confession is the resolve to amend one's life of the former sin. In view of the high value placed on confession of sin in the Bible, the thrust of its message is that confession without a sincere desire to actively change former lifestyles or wrong behavior is insincere and meaningless.

In the process of marital reconciliation, partners must not only confess their failures to one another, but their lives must also show that there is a clean break with past deeds which were once harmful to the marriage. Once a couple has experienced the cleansing and healing accompanied with open confession, there must also be sincere resolve to amend their marriage from similar errors in the future.

Integrity Therapy places due emphasis on the concept of restitution in the process of reconciliation. With the i emphasis that Integrity Therapy places on restitution, I find that this concept is closely relating with the biblical concept of reconciliation. (How do we put back what was taken by irresponsible and wrong behavior in the marriage relationship). In conclusion, confession embraces the principles of openness and responsibility for personal wareness of wrong behavior. These two princi ples provide 'an avenue for integrity and reconciliation in marriage. When this occurs, marriages have a great hope for future harmony and joy.

Chapter V

REVIEW AND REFLECT

Well, you've made it through four chapters... Congratulations. Now we are going to take a pause to review and reflect on the principles previously outlined to better assimilate these concepts.

I understand that some of these principles of theological and psychological thought have not been easy to grasp. Nevertheless, I hope that these principles for reconciliation in marriage made sense to you. I like it when people read a book, sit back and say, "Now that makes sense!" When I became an instructor in the Parent Project, (a ten-week course for parenting difficult children), I said to myself, "everything that I was taught made perfect sense!"

I can guarantee that this chapter will be helpful. It's always good to review the last four chapters so that you can look forward to the conclusion of this book. So, in review, when I entitled this book, "Reigniting the Fire", I was always interested to observe people's reaction. More often than not, people were intrigued because the reference to reignite the fire led them to think about sex in marriage. Well, you'll have to wait until I get to the last chapter. Sex and mutual affection are a very important part in the process of reconciliation.

The Garden of Eden

There are many things aboutthe Garden of Eden that remain unexplained to me. It is no mystery that we accept that the triune God created all of creation. But the biblical record still leaves out answers to many mysteries. God said, "It is not good for the man to be alone. I will make a helper suitable for him". (Genesis 2:18) The first question that comes to my mind is how long Adam lived alone in the garden before the Lord decided that a companion was needed. Adam's partner was indeed created but at what price? His companion would be a woman. Woman was made from Adam's body. So, God anesthetized Adam and performed a deep surgery out of Adam's rib, God created a beautiful woman. With God nothing is impossible.

Here's another mystery. What did Adam think and feel when he saw his new and beautiful companion? Even though the bible does not share our happy couples' reactions, nevertheless, they both likely were exceptionally beautiful.

Eve was her name. After Adam met Eve, he wrote the first love poem: "Now this is bone from my bones and flesh of my flesh, she will be called 'woman' because she was taken from out of man" (Genesis 2:23).

After God created Eve, He said, "they shall become one flesh". (Genesis 2:24). And then the bible says that Adam and his wife were "both naked and felt no shame". (Genesis 2:25). Now there becomes an astonishing and amazing thought. Did our happy couple enjoy sexuality freely, openly, without any shame? It was God's design for our happy couple to enjoy the freedom of God-ordained sexuality. Sex was experience in total freedom, total bliss, total love, and perfect unity. In the perfect garden our happy parents relished the truth of true unity. Their sexuality completed the mystery of the two becoming one flesh. Becoming 'one flesh' was accomplished and experienced in this beautiful paradise.

Again, we do not know how long our happy couple were in this state of bliss. The bible does tell us that their time in paradise did not last. Woe to us all! Time in this wonderful garden was lost due to their disobedience and rebellion. They had been given only one rule: God said, "You must not eat from the tree of knowledge of good and evil, for when you eat from it you will certainly die". (Genesis 2:17) Another mystery—How did this magnificent creature ever gain entrance into this gorgeous paradise? How is it that this evil creature tempted our first parents? And so, just as in our present culture, the two were duped by the serpent and they were told the first lie. The evil tempter said, "Did

God really say, 'You must not eat from any tree in the garden'?" "If you eat fruit, you will not die," the serpent said to the woman. "For God knows that when you eat from it your eyes will be opened, and you will be like God, knowing good and evil." (Genesis3:1,4-5) The serpent's suggestion of doubt opened a door where Adam and Eve questioned their trust in God. And so, they broke God's one and only rule, and the bible says, "their eyes were open, they were naked, and they experienced shame for the first time". (Genesis 3:7) And to make a long story short, they were banished from the Garden, and no one was ever allowed to enter the Garden again. God established his angels to guard 'The Way' to the Tree of Life.

I hope this gives you a huge hint of how great was God's love. If the Way to the Garden was blocked, Jesus said to his disciples, "No one comes to the Father except through Me. I am the "Way," the Truth and the Life". In the Garden, our happy couple experienced truth, freedom, openness, and life! And so, the Lord gave the couple a profound promise, a mighty gift and a bold prophecy. God said to Adam, "I will put enmity (a state of being hostile or opposed to one another) between you and the Woman". (Genesis 3:15) As a result of their rebellion, there will be an ongoing power struggle and a profound ongoing and terrible conflict. Not good news for our happy couple. Not good news for us either. Nevertheless, God gave them a promise and a hope. Your offspring from many generations to come will bring forth a man. A beautiful and kind man, Jesus. This good man will bring an end to Satan's power. God said thatthis man, Jesus will stomp on the Serpent's head and kill him. The Serpent will have minimal power and merely bruise the heal of this good man, Jesus. So, as time went on, circumstances in this world became increasingly hostile, wicked and cruel. There was a time when the world became so evil that God regretted his own creation. God called forth Noah to build an ark for the salvation of the human race.

Everything else that He created was destroyed. After Noah Abraham soon enters the scene. Abraham was the father of all believers. The evil persisted, but God said to Abraham, "Fear not. I am your shield, and your ancestors will be very great". (Genesis 15:1). Abraham believed that God would be faithful. In their old age, God gave Abraham a beautiful son whose name was Isaac. As time went on, the world continued to deteriorate. And God told Abraham to take his only and beloved son' to a high mountain to kill him and offer him as a sacrifice to God. Unlike the first Adam, Abraham was obedient. Abraham brought his son Isaac to the top of the mountain, and just as Abraham was about to slay his son, God intervened. An angel stopped this horiffic murderous act. God provided a substitute and stopped the drama. Isaac was not sacrificed, and God blessed Abraham for his obedience.

Israel in Egypt

With the passage of time, God's people were held captive in bondage to a cruel pharaoh in Egypt. God raised up the Hebrew Moses to deliver his people and brought the Israelites into the desert after miraculously crossing the Red Sea. This is very significant. God called Moses to the top of Mt Sinai to give the people the Ten Commandments. As you read this story i hope you begin to see how events are wonderfully encapsulated in a marriage ceremony. Israel was to cleanse themselves before the Lord and clothe themselves in pure white garments. The vows of this wedding are clear. Moses came down from the mountain with the Ten Commandments, these commandments are the new and sacred Wedding Vows. The people agreed to the terms of these marital vows. They promised to keep these vows. At that very moment, God and Israel formed a new marital relationship!

Israel promised obedience and God promised his presence and protection. From that point on, we have the biblical analogy of God being the husband, and Israel being His wife. Repeatedly through out the bible we see stories of God's faithfulness and Israel's rebellion. God was faithful, but Israel was disobedient. After numerous warnings, works of great miracles and demonstrations of both kindness and anger, the Lord was brought to a grave decision. He could no longer keep Israel as his wife and wrote her a legal Bill of Divorce. In the book of Hosea, we read these unhappy words," Plead with your mother (Israel), plead with her, for she is not my wife, and I (the Lord) am not her husband". (Hosea 2:2) Nevertheless, the promise of a new marriage was still within the reach of God's grace, kindness and love.

The New Covenant and Bridal Imagery

The Bible tells us, that at the designated and appropriate time, Jesus, the only Son of God, came into the world. He was conceived by the Holy Spirit and born of a virgin woman. He suffered intensely during his lifetime. He performed great and mighty miracles and alas, he was cruelly murdered at the hands of the wicked people. He suffered and endured the awful and unbearable crucifixion. He was buried and with great power rose again from the dead. The resurrection guaranteed that the marriage to his new bride the church was solid. Here Jesus became the great and Mighty Bridegroom. Through Christ's resurrection, the new covenant was now open to all people, to all nations and to all races. Can anyone wrap their mind around this astonishing work of atonement, this is why I believe that only through bridal imagery can we fully begin to understand the scope and meaning of the work of Christ on the cross.

The culmination of Jesus' death and resurrection is the New Covenant that God implemented through Christ, fulfilling the promise that God spoke to Adam and Eve in the Garden.

Before I conclude this chapter, I want to share some thoughts with you with the words of Christ in John 14:6-7. It was just before the Passover Feast (the Last Supper), Jesus knew that the time had come for Him to leave this world and go to the Father. During this passionate discourse, Jesus gave his disciples many wonderful messages about His ministry and his upcoming sacrifice. Jesus said: "I am the Way, the Truth, and the Life. No one comes to the father except through Me. If you really knew Me, you would know the Father as well. From now on, you do know the Father, and you have seen the Father through Me".

Friends, this is both a very simple truth, and it is also a very difficult concept to understand. On the one hand, Jesus is saying that the only way for reconciliation with God the Father is to come through Jesus.

On the other hand, I also want you to remember and recognize the fact that when our happy couple, Adam and Eve, were in the garden of total bliss and perfect communion with God: they were complete and happy. But they sinned and disobeyed and were driven out of the garden into a very cruel world. The Bible states, that 'The Way' back into the garden was blocked and guarded for all time. In Genesis 3:24, we read, "After he drove the happy couple out, He placed on the east side of the Garden of Eden, cherubim and a flaming sword, flashing back and forth, to guard 'The Way' to the Tree of Life". When I think of reconciliation, I cannot help but think about the Tree of Life. The real significance of the Tree of Life is incomprehensible; nevertheless, the Book of Revelation reveals more aboutthe Tree of Life. In Revelation 4, John was given a vision and John says, "there before me was a door standing open in heaven". An open door is significant for the word, 'Way'. In Revelation, Chapter 22, the reference to the Tree of Life is this: John says, "then the Angel showed me the River of the Water of Life, as clear as crystal, flowing from the throne of God and of the Lamb. This river was flowing down the middle of the street and on each side of the river (an island?) stood the tree of life. On each side of the river stood the Tree of Life with the tree bearing 12 crops of fruits, yielding its fruit every month. And the leaves of the tree are for the healing of the nations. Now that's a beautiful picture of a beautiful tree. There's another tree... that leads to the open door of heaven and to the Tree of Life that was banished for all time. That tree was the tree that Jesus hung on and for us, the Tree of Life was the old rugged cross. When saying that He is 'The Way' back into the garden, the gates which were previously guarded, and are reopened to a multitude of people. Is it possible for us to comprehend what really happened at the crucifixion and resurrection of Jesus? The one thing I know, is that reconciliation is open to all, and God's love is all encompassing and never gives up.

I believe that it's important to note, that Jesus is now the new Bridegroom to His church, the bride. It is also important to note that the bride is not yet fully married to Jesus but will await the coming of the Groom when the final wedding takes place as mentioned in the Book of Revelation. When Jesus was on earth and at the Last Supper,

He said to his disciples, "I go to prepare a place for you. And if I go and prepare a place for you, I will come again and receive you unto myself; that is where I am, there you may be also". (John 14:2,3). Nobody knows when Jesus is coming back to receive His bride. The bible tells us that only the Father knows when Jesus is coming back to claim His bride. And then, at that time, all things will be complete, and the wedding feast will commence. Welcome to the Party!

The Biblical imagery of the bride (the church) and the bride groom Gesus christ) and marriage between a husband and wife makes perfect sense. For sure there is a mystery here on both levels. On the one hand Paul writes in Eph 5: 31-32 "For this reason a man will leave his father and mother and cleave to his wife and the two will become one flesh. Then Paul says this is a profound mystery-". Then Paul adds, "I am also talking about Christ and the church".

In the high priestly prayer of Jesus, Jesus also writes of the mystery of the church and Jesus becoming one flesh. In John 14: 19-20, Jesus says, "Because I live, you also will live. On that day you will realize that I am in my father (Christ's resurrection) and you are in me and i am in you... He who loves me will be loved by my father and I too will love him and show myself to him. (church /bride)-in John 15, Jesus continues to speak of this divine unity by speaking of the vine and the branches. Jesus says, "I am the true vine, you are already clean (Jesus' atonement and reconciliation) because of the word I have spoken to you. Remain in me and i will remain in you. I am the vine, and you are the branches. As the father has loved me so have i love you. Now remain in my love. Of you obey my command (love God/ Love your neighbor) you will remain in my love just as I have obeyed my father's commands and remain in his love. I have told you this that my joy may be in you and your joy may be complete!

There you have it! The mystery of the two becoming one and the promise of true joy. Joy is the goal of both spiritual untiy with Christ and the joy of marriage between a husband and a wife! That is the fire that needs to be reignited on a continued level in marriage. Both human and divine! Finally, Paul writes in Romans 16. "Now to him who is able to establish you by my gospel (Good news) and the proclamation of Jesus Christ according to the revelation of the mystery hidden for long ages past!"

In our relationship with Jesus Christ it is always growing, changing, developing, renewing and becoming more intimate. Our relationship continues to produce fruit guided by the joy of Lord Jesus Christ.

One of my favorite paintings is Jesus' walking with the two men on the road to Emas—the three men are walking on a beautiful path surrounded by large trees with sunlight breaking through the leaves and branches. You can see they are in a deep and interesting conversation. Two men did not know they were talking to the resurrected Jesus—As they approached their home they invited Jesus for dinner—As Jesus broke bread he disappears, and the two men are astonished and knew that they were in the presence of Jesus—Then with great emotion they said "Did not our hearts burn with in us? "Yes, they did, and it was the presence of Jesus the dignified the fire in their hearts—That in a great story of our divine relationship with Jesus -

So, you see that there can be fire both on the divine level and on the human level in marriage—Marriage between a husband and wife can also be a dynamic, ever growing and ever changing in a positive direction of freedom love, unity and joy.

This is good news for reconciled married couples. - I wish I could say this is true for everyone and unfortunately there is bad news. I have to bring a balance to the truth of human marriage. The bad news is that overall marriage is on the decline—More young couples are not seeing the need to marry—and unfortunately there are good reasons to support this reality—I will list them now:

- the average years that a marriage last in the U.S. is 8 years!

- The average rate of divorce in U.S. is 50%

- Divorce rate in California is 2 of 3 marriages end in Divorce

- California is a no-fault state for divorce!

- Most divorces are caused by economic problems with an adequate income!

- Most common reason for divorce

  » Marital infidelity

  » Frequent fighting/ arguing

  » Lack of commitment and communication

  » In maturity

  » Substance abuse (alcohol, drugs, use of pornography by both men and woman)

  » Different goals, priorities, lifestyles and values -

  » Domestic violence and physical abuse

  » Lack of religion affiliation

  » History of parental divorces

Nevertheless, it's not all bad news either

- Average divorce rate is declining

- People are delaying marriage—due to financial reasons and career choices.

- People are "pickier" in choosing a marriage partner

- People have seen firsthand parents struggle and don't want to repeat

- Disputes over child custody arrangements are too costly emotionally and financially and thus couples are choosing not to divorce

- Marriage and parental counseling in on the upward trend—

- Finally, there is a strong spiritual revival happening in the United States of America and around the world

I think it is clear that one purpose of marriage is to "procreate" and "multiply" in order to "subdue the earth"—we are commanded to continue the line of human life populate the world. Allow me to be clear not all people are destined for marriage St. Paul said it was better for him to remain single than marry. Should you be one who chooses to marry there in another purpose—that purpose is to thwart off loneliness Ecclesiastes says two are better than one!"—Another purpose in marriage is that God created us for satisfying our own sexual arousal for our own pleasure, intimacy—there is no need to be ashamed of this either. What matters is the decision we make and the steps we take to control our sexual urges.

There is a difference between what is good and what is distorted. There is plenty in our culture that can lead to a distorted sexuality. I think it is true that if in marriage there is wrong behavior on either spouse, there will also be a distorted negative result in the sexual bond of marriage. If there is distrust, fear and anxiety in the marriage relationship it will no doubt also have a negative effect on the healthy sexual life of that marriage. The lack of healthy sexual relations could lead to an unsatisfying marriage. But this is not always the case. I believe that the lack of sex in marriage can lead to estrangement and distance in the marriage. There is a possibility that it can open the door to restlessness and temptation. Nevertheless, there is with all spouses there is a deep need and powerful drive to come together as one flesh.

One of the confessional standards centers around the teaching of the Christian reformed church. Heidelberg Catechism regarding and encompasses the various issues regarding adultery. The issue of adultery has far reaching moral issues for all people.

The various issues regarding adultery center around and are not limited to:

- Pre-marital sex

- Extra marital sex

- Polyamore (sex with more than one partner)

- Pornography

- Homosexual sex

- Sexual violence both within and outside of marriage

On the positive side i think it is important for my readers to know that i believe that marriage must be between a male and female in unity and freedom. —and of course it is always best if both marital parties are believers in Jesus.

Chapter VI

Reignite the fire

Choosing the title "Reignite the Fire" was very intentional. I hope in the proceeding chapters I have been successful in helping you to better understand that fire needs to be on both a divine and human level. Whenever I tell people about the title of my book "Reignite the Fire"—their response is WOW! I cannot wait to read it. There must be some sex in this book somewhere!

There is a really old book and one of my favorite books entitles "come to the party" by Karl Olson (copyright 1972). Our family celebrated a party to end all parties everywhere! Saturday April 1, 2023, my granddaughter Kaylee Elizabeth de Falkenberg was married to Austin Jones at a winery in Temecula, California. Let me say without bias, it was by far the most beautiful wedding ever! I have attended a number of weddings in my life (both as a guest and an officiant) this wedding was the best! Three days prior to the wedding it rained in Southern California continuously! On Saturday morning the sun was shining brightly with azure, blue skies! Off in the distance was the absolutely beautiful view of the snow caped San Gorgonio Mountain range. God could not have made a more magnificent and majestic view for the happy couple. Jesus was present! The sweet Holy Spirit was present in a gentle wisp of a breeze to keep Kaylee and Austin and their guests very comfortable! The wedding message was great. The sacred vows and the exchanging of rings were most sacred! The banquet was most exquisite and delicious-the food was served hot and tasty-the parental toasts were beautiful and emotional. There were tears and laughter all tied into one grand theme of a party! Finally, the D.J. said "all dance!" Wow we danced the night away! Overall, it was a great party!

In his book "Come to the Party" Karl Olsen writes that there are just too many wonderful things to say about the last great wedding banquet.

In summary it is basically a book about Jesus inviting all people to his grand party. In the last chapter of the book Karl Olsen writes "Because Jesus hosted a party in which he himself was the bread and wine. The food and the wine were given to even the "deniers" and "betrayers." Because they can eat and drink, we all have the right and the courage to come to this party. We can be with him and with all his "blessed" and unblessed children forever! So why do I mention a party when I talk about reigniting the fire? Well, when there is unity, love, freedom and understanding no marriage is complete unless there is healthy and good sex. Good sex is a party for sure!

You know the old song-love and marriage go together like a horse and carriage-you can't have one without the other—for this chapter I would like to change the words to this song—"sex and marriage go together like a horse and carriage-you can't have one without the other."

I have been struggling with myself to write this last chapter. I have been resisting it. You must hear my confession again—"I was scared." Nancy and I grew up in Minnesota! Writers are bitter, cold with wild blizzards and tons of snow! Winter seems to last an eternity! The only solution is to become a "snowbird" escape to the Sun City Arizona—that's exactly what Nancy's parents did! Nancy and I grew up in the Christian Reformed Church. There is a Christian Reformed Church in Sun City Arizona. Nancy's parents faithfully attended this church. On one particular Sunday morning the retired pastor preached a sermon on the seventh commandment "Thou shall not commit adultery." It was a sermon that Nancy and I will never forget—"He began his sermon by saying, "This subject always made him nervous. I wish I didn't have to preach on this subject at all! He continued, "when I was ordained, I vowed to preach on the whole counsel of God and all of God's word. The good pastor began his sermon with, "when it comes to this subject, I even hate to say the word sex!" He said the word so softly that it almost sounded seductive! Then he spoke of pre-marital sex. He said "Having premarital sex is like a half-baked cake. When it comes out of the oven it looks beautiful on the outside but when you eat into it, it is all wet and gooey on the inside. It's not good at all!" Then he went on to talk about conversations that are sexually inappropriate. He said, "when you have visitors to your home you don't bring them down basement and show them the boiler that burns coal to heat the house! No, you bring them to your beautiful living room and have pleasant clean conversations!" When we all returned home and visited around our dinner table, we all fondly recalled many of his funny illustrations—with great laughter. To be honest it is probably the one sermon I will never forget!

Unlike our retired pastor, I want to affirm to you that sex is good, beautiful, and necessary to a restored marriage. In fact, the more sex you have with your spouse the better the marriage will be! After all, God created humans with the gift of sexuality. At the very beginning of creation God created man and woman. Then he said that everything he created was very good! As you know, there is more to sex than just intercourse. Just outside of Philadelphia there is an Amish village called "Intercourse" and of course gift shops cannot keep enough shirts and sweatshirts in stock. When we were kids, we would always laugh when we sang the hymn "They were having intercourse with their beloved ones at Hearth and Board!" The meaning of course was that they were having hearty discussions on many matters. It's very clear then that healthy sexuality is not limited to just sexual intercourse.

However, there is a special and unique bond that is established in sexual intercourse. It is a bond of deep love, unity, and intimacy. It is indeed a deep form of "connecting." The author Larry Crabb writes, "when two people connect, when their beings intersect closely as two bodies during intercourse, something is poured out of one and into the other that has the power to heal the soul of its deepest wounds and restore it to health. The one who receives experiences the joy of being healed. The one who gives knows the even greater joy of being used to being a healer. Something good is in the heart of each of Gods children that is more powerful than everything that is bad. It's there, waiting to be released to work its magic-" This is of course a great mystery. Saint Paul writes "when a man and woman become one it is a great mystery.

Jesus said, "Father may they become one as we are one." Jesus also said, "you are no longer slaves—a servant does not care what his master is doing—He continues, "You are no longer servants, but you are friends." A longtime ago, I became friends with Jesus. A friend is a very close and intimate relationship—you can tell a friend anything and a friend "loves at all times." (Proverbs 17: 17) I am going to switch gears for a minute and tell you one more of my friendships with Jesus. The last only time I walked through labyrinth was at Saint Mary's and Joseph retreat center in San Pedro, California. I had a most amazing experience with my friend Jesus—he walked behind me; he walked with me, and he walked ahead of me. If you have never walked the labyrinth, I highly recommend it. There are some sharp U-turns. These U-turns led me to numerous awareness of my need for repentance. Jesus was always there to listen and forgive. Then at times the labyrinth had very long walkways. For me, this part of the labyrinth was scary-where will this path take me and what lies ahead? Then my friend Jesus walked ahead of me with a flaming and powerful sword ready to slay any enemy! When I came to the final part of the labyrinth—the very center—there Jesus and I stood quietly together after my long journey. While in this sacred circle of trust I heard Jesus say, "you did not choose me, but I chose you!" That experience was an amazing spiritual moment. I don't think I have ever felt so close to my friend Jesus ever. I really felt one with Jesus with a peace that passed all understanding—I hated to leave and rejoin our group, nevertheless Jesus left and said, "call on me anytime and I will come to you!"

Finally, sometime ago my pastor Reverend Don Porter, opened Gods word to Jesus high priestly prayer. Words to his disciples—"it is necessary for me to leave you, and I am going to prepare a place for you. If I go, I will come back to receive you—I cannot tell you how many times I have heard these words. But for the first time it struck home—death has no hold on me. I can't say I'm looking forward to my own death. I now have no fear of going through the valley of death. When it is my time to leave this earth my good friend Jesus will come to me and receive me as his beautiful bride—there it is the mystery—we are one! When couples come together sexually, that is also a mystery of deep unity. There is so much more to be said about sexual intimacy and marital reconciliation—I think the best way to continue marital reconciliation is to participate in good sex as often as two married people can. Couples can experience sexual passion when they can both discover each other's "attractiveness." Emotional and physical attraction is a good way to find their way back to love with passion and desire! One more thing, couples who experience reconciliation must experience sexual freedom to discover new and exciting ways of showing sexual pleasure. This is a wonderful way of showing renewed love! A renewed marital relationship is so exciting especially when this renewed relationship is anchored in positive fidelity. Sex without boundaries leads to disunity and bondage! Marital fidelity obligates both spouses to seek one another's independence and freedom. Satisfying sexual relations within marriage leads to the renewal of the mystery—of love. The Good Lord has given us all one life to live. If Gods purpose for you is to be married and reconciliation is part of that purpose, then joy is just around the corner. Within the sacred bonds of a renewed marriage there will be novel sexual initiatives, creative approaches to healthy sexual experiences and unexpected sexual surprises that are all blessed by God. It is a wonderous thing for couples to be reunited. This is the joy of committed love, and the happy couple can set their passions on fire once again. This is God's design for husbands and wives to live in the total freedom that only Christ can provide. After all God created sex, so let us rejoice and be glad in it! First Timothy 4:4 St. Paul writes, "for everything created by God is good and nothing is to be rejected if it is received with thanksgiving." Please receive God's gift of sexuality with great thanksgiving and joy.

Conclusion

I have one more confession—I am getting kind of turned on just writing about all this sex!I have to remind myself that sex is a good thing. Yes indeed it is. Well, we have come to the end! Reigniting the fire happens on many levels of human experience and marriage—this book is my work of love for all of you. My publisher asked me, "why did you write this book and what are your goals for your readers?' Very good questions. I wrote this book because I have a desire to help those whose marriages are in need of reconciliation. Nancy and I have been married now for 56 years. Without a doubt she is my very best friend. If you and your spouse are no longer friends, you can still become friends once again. I need you to apply the many principles that I have outlined in this book. These are very sound biblical and psychological truths for you and your spouse. In addition, I strongly recommend that you find a marriage counselor who is well seasoned and experienced. Marriage counseling is challenging.

Friendship in marriage is a good goal for you and your spouse. It takes time—don't rush it. To be friends with your spouse and friends with the almighty Lord, the King of Creation is one amazing miracle! The greatest miracle of all is that we are all invited to the King's great wedding banquet! It's going to be a grand party, trust me.

One of my reasons for writing this book is that there is a great need for marital reconciliation in our present culture. Marriage is in big trouble. If your marriage is good, then it can be made better. Good, better, best never let it rest. I am still waiting for the day when a couple comes to my office and says, "Our marriage is good, and we just want to make it better!" It hasn't happened yet!

If your marriage is just not going to be reconciled because of irreconcilable differences, then God bless you. Divorce is never a good thing. It is emotionally, physically, and financially very costly—divorce causes many ripples that affect family, children and friends and community. I have seen it and it's very painful. Just believe that God has a plan and a purpose for your new and next adventure. St. Paul was right when he wrote, "now we see through a glass darkly, but then we shall see Christ clearly, face to face. Now I only know in part, then I shall fully know, even as I am fully known. Now these three remain faith, hope, and love shall always abide but the greatest of these is "Love" Amen.

Bibliography

Bailey, D. S. The mystery of love and marriage, New York: Harper and Row, 1952.

Barth, K. On marriage. Vol. 3. Philadelphia: Fortress Press, 1968.

Batey, R. A. New Testament nuptial imagery. Leiden: Brill, 1971.

Batey, R. A. The union of Christ and the church. New Testament Studies, April, 1967, pp. 270-281.

Buchanan, J. Analogy: A guide to truth and an aid to faith. Edinburgh: T. & T. Clark, 1867.

Cahn, Z. The philosophy of Judaism. New York: Macmillan, 1962.

Calvin, J. Commentaries of the twelve minor prophets. Vol. 1 Hosea. Grand Rapids: Wm. B. Eerdmans, 1950.

Chavasse, C. The bride of Christ. London: Religious Book Club, 1939.

Clinebell, H. J., & Clinebell, C. H. The intimate marriage. New York: Harper and Row, 1970.

Cobham, D. Covenant. In A. Richardson (Ed.), A theological wordbook of the Bible. New York: Macmillan, 1951.

Cole, W. G. Sex and love in the Bible. New York: Associated Press, 1959.

Crabb, Larry. The Marriage Builder. Grand Rapids: Zondervan Publishing House. 1982.

Dodd, C. H. The apostolic preaching and its developments. London: Holder and Stoughton, 1936.

Dodd, C. H. Epistle of Paul to the Romans. New York: Harper and Row, 1931.

Dodd, C. H. The message of the epistle Ephesians. Expository Times, 1933, 45, 60-66.

Drakeford, J. W. Integrity Therapy. Nashville: Broadman Press, 1967.

Glasser, W. Reality Therapy. New York: Harper and Row, 1965.

Greidanus, S. Sola Scripture. New York: Van Kampen, 1970.

Hendricksen, W. Bible survey. Grand Rapids: Baker Book House, 1947.

Hiltner, S. Pastoral counseling. Nashville: Abingdon Cokesbury Press, 1949.

Hubbard, D. A. The knowledge of God in Hosea. Unpublished master's thesis, Fuller Theological Seminary, Pasadena, California, 1954.

Hubbard, D. A. With bands of love. Grand Rapids: Wm. B. Eerdmans, 1968.

Lampe, G. W. H., & Woolcombe, K. J. Essays on typology. Naperville, Ill.: Alec R. Allenson, 1957.

Moore, G. F. Judaism. Vols. 1, 2, 3. Cambridge: Harvard University Press, 1946.

Moore, G. F. The literature of the Old Testament. London: Oxford University Press, 1948.

Mowrer, O. H. Integrity groups: Basic principles and objectives. The Counseling Psychologist, 1972, 1(2), 7-33.

Mowrer, O. H. The new group therapy. Princeton: Van Nostrand, 1964.

Oden, T. C. Kerygma and counseling. Philadelphia: Westminster Press, 1966.

Richardson, A. A theological wordbook of the Bible. New York: Macmillan, 1951.

Robinson, H. W. The religious ideas of the Old Testament. London: Gerald Duckworth and Co., 1952.

Rowley, H. H. The faith of Israel. Philadelphia: Westminster Press, 19 6.

Rowley, H. H. Men of God. London: Thomas Nelson and Sons, 1963.

Rowley, H. H. The relevance of the apocalyptic. 3d ed. London: Lutherworth Press, 1964.

Smedes, L. All things made new. Grand Rapids: Wm. B. Eerdmans, 1970.

Snaith, N. H. Amos, Hosea, and Micah. London: Epworth Press, 1956.

Snaith, N. H. Distinctive ideas of the Old Testament. London: Epworth Press, 1950.

Thielicke, H. Theological ethics. Philadelphia: Fortress Press, 1960.

Thielicke, H. The ethics of sex. Trans. by J. W. Doberstein. New York: Harper and Row, 1964.

Von Rad, G. Old Testament theology. Vol. 1. New York: Harper and Row, 1965.

Ward, J.M. Hosea: A theological commentary. New York: Harper and Row, 1966.

Credits

I have heard it said, "you alone must do it but you can't do it alone". Even though I did write this book it could not have been completed with friends who helped me. I would like to thank my manager from Blue Ink Media Solutions Mr. Drake Collins. Drake only wishes the best for me.

I would like to thank my friend Nathan Little for his expert typing and editing. What a computer whiz he is!

Also I want to thank my Pastoral Assistant, Miss Vicky Montgomery. Vicky is a grace filled perfectionist!

Finally I want to thank my beautiful and friendly neighbor Mrs. Rochelle Mendez. Rochelle typed my last chapter and finished the book. Together we knocked it out of the park.

Dr. Eric Evenhuis.